A GOD FOR ALL SEASONS

A God
For All Seasons

*Encouragement for Women
who Juggle their Lives*

SUE HAYDON-KNOWELL

MONARCH
BOOKS

Mill Hill, London & Grand Rapids, Michigan

First published by Monarch Books in the UK in 2002,
Concorde House, Grenville Place,
Mill Hill, London NW7 3SA.

Distributed by:
UK: STL, PO Box 300, Kingstown Broadway, Carlisle,
Cumbria CA3 0QS;
USA: Kregel Publications, PO Box 2607
Grand Rapids, Michigan 49501.

ISBN 1 85424 480 9

British Library Cataloguing Data
A catalogue record for this book is available
from the British Library.

Book design and production for the publishers by
Bookprint Creative Services
P.O. Box 827, BN21 3YJ, England.
Printed in Great Britain.

To my daughters Amy, Leigh and Katie
and my granddaughters
Anna and Juliet
with love

CONTENTS

FOREWORD

In the last 50 years, the world has changed enormously for women. After the upheaval of World War Two, women tried to settle back into normality by creating homes and sustaining families as their mothers had done before them. But things had changed. Money, and many commodities, were scarce. Many had lost husbands; many had tasted working outside the home in munitions factories or other forms of work. Hardship, loss and instability led to cynicism and questioning of the old order.

Then, in the sixties, rebellion erupted against old values which were pushed aside in a climate of sexual freedom made possible by the availability of the contraceptive pill. As the decades pass, divorce has become frequent, and family life fragmented; single parenthood no longer carries a stigma; and most women work outside the home.

Girls born in the closing decades of the old millennium face a volatile world, seething with conflicting ideas. Women of all ages find themselves caught up in circumstances beyond their control, often bewildered and frustrated, sometimes angry.

How are Christian women to respond to today's pressures? Sue Haydon-Knowell has written an important book, which helps women to identify their problems and their reactions, and deal with them constructively in the light of the Bible's teaching.

This book is worth buying for the third chapter alone, dealing with the issue of singleness. There is a dearth of honest writing for Christian single women that is truth-based yet practical. She tackles it forthrightly, calling a spade a spade, and helping women get a clear perspective on their situation. The chapters on marriage and motherhood are also approached with refreshing honesty and insight, and the whole book is peppered with vivid illustrations and anecdotes from the lives of real women. She writes vigorously with a lack of compromise and yet with humour and compassion.

This book will be a useful tool for women at every season of life.

Wendy Virgo

INTRODUCTION

After nearly three decades as a pastor's wife, I have known plenty of women "with attitudes" (and had a few attitudes myself!). This book is for all the women, young and old, who have shared my life. Some of my friends have sailed smoothly through, from marriage to menopause and beyond, with very little "stormy weather". But they are few. Most of us experience battles and struggles as we live through the different seasons of our lives.

As I write this, I am thinking about a wedding I will attend next Saturday. My friend Sheila's daughter is the last of their children to get married, so for Sheila a new season of life will begin. She had an unexpected "change of season" when her husband was made redundant last year. How will she cope with the changes?

Like the English weather, our lives can change without warning from sunshine to storms, and sometimes our reactions to change can surprise and shock us. Resentment and negative attitudes can pull us down and we fail to acknowledge God's sovereignty and love. As Christian women we want Jesus to be Lord in our lives; we want to experience his peace and joy in our marriages, our homes and our workplaces; we want to relate well with our families, our friends, our neighbours and our work colleagues. But sometimes we can't seem to live the "Jesus way". We find ourselves saying with the apostle Paul, "What I want to do I do not do, but what I hate I do" (Romans 7:15).

This book looks at the attitudes which can hold us back from a lifestyle of fulfilment and growth in our knowledge and love of God through the different seasons of life. Only he can change our attitudes so that we are "transformed by the renewing of [our] mind" (Romans 12:2). The mind is where all our attitudes begin and take root, affecting all our reactions, choices and relationships from the moment we are born.

In the following chapters we will see how to be "made new in the attitude[s] of [our] minds" (Ephesians 4:23), so that we can live through the seasons of our lives with freedom, creativity and increasing maturity.

Many of my friends have contributed their experiences to this book. I have seen God work in their lives to bring change as they have allowed him to do so. If you are in a "season" of life which is proving a struggle because your attitudes have not changed to fit that season; if you are holding on to the past in a way which prevents you growing in the present, I pray that this book will show you a way forward into the life and peace which comes from having your mind "controlled by the Spirit [of God]" (Romans 8:6).

I want to thank all the friends who have allowed me to use their stories here. I have changed some of their names in order to protect their confidentiality. My thanks also to Eagle, the publishers of Sue Ashdown's book *Till Death Us Do Part?*, for allowing me to quote part of her book in chapter 3.

Scripture quotations in the book are from the *New International Version* of the Bible.

CHAPTER ONE

ATTITUDES AND ANTIDOTES

As I write, it is a glorious July morning, and through my window I can see people walking along the road dressed for sunshine. Shorts and a T-shirt are wonderful gear for a sunny summer's day in the garden or on the beach. But a person who refused to wear anything but shorts and a T-shirt through the autumn and into the cold weather of winter would suffer serious consequences. She would suffer physically because of the cold and she would suffer emotionally because of the painful situation the weather had caused for her. No doubt she would become upset and angry. Eventually, as the weather became more severe, her cries would become pitiful as her limbs froze. If she refused to put on warmer clothes, her attitude of non-acceptance of the change in the weather would ultimately kill her – and the people around her, who had offered her warm sweaters, trousers and boots, would be saddened.

This is an extreme metaphor, but all around us there are people who are holding on to entrenched attitudes and refusing to change with the "seasons" of their lives. A few weeks ago I was shopping in our local supermarket when I saw a pair of twins. They were dressed identically in matching skirts, coats and shoes. Their hairstyles, handbags and even their facial expressions were exactly the same. Sometimes twins look cute when they are dressed alike, especially when they are toddlers, but these twins were in their mid-50s. They were women who had obviously found their identities in "being twins" when they were children and apparently had never felt secure enough as individual adults to leave their "twin" identity behind. But at their age it didn't look cute, only rather sad.

Changing attitudes as we grow

As we move on in life, we will experience change. We grow older (unlike the hero of the *Just William* books, who remains forever eleven years old!). Our tastes change; our circumstances and relationships change. Our children will not remain toddlers – they will become teenagers and then adults. Our attitudes and behaviour toward them must change; if this does not happen, our relationships with them will become strained and difficult. We cannot tell a 20-year-old son or daughter to be home by ten o'clock!

"Attitude" can be defined as a mind-set which produces thought, action and reaction. As we mature as women and as Christians, we must leave immature attitudes behind us and embrace new ones. Sometimes this can be "scary"; we wonder whether we will lose something of our selfhood in the process of change. But we belong to God's family, and his aim for us is to "conform as to the likeness of his Son" (Romans 8:29). Jesus' relationship with his heavenly Father and with his own disciples was not hindered by wrong attitudes. He was totally free to obey whatever his Father called him to do, whether it was healing a sick man, rebuking the Pharisees or speaking life-changing words to a Samaritan woman at a well. Changing our attitudes to conform to his will bring us gain, not loss.

Our attitudes affect our lives

This is not a "how-to" book about singleness, marriage, parenting or growing old. Neither is it about premenstrual syndrome, hormones or hot flushes! There are many books available which deal with these matters in excellent detail. This book is about *attitudes*; it looks at ways of changing heart-attitudes which may be hindering our emotional and spiritual growth in the particular season of life through which we are living. In Romans 12:2 the apostle Paul talks about our need to be "transformed by the renewing of [our] mind." This renewing of our mind happens when we co-operate with God and allow him to change our attitudes; this will then produce change in our choices, behaviour and relationships.

Some years ago I was praying for a dear friend of mine who was being held back in her spiritual life by some entrenched attitudes. As I prayed, God gave me a picture. I saw my friend sitting in a prison cell, chained to the wall. Strangely, the door of the cell stood open. I looked at the heavy metal chain around my friend's ankle and followed the links up to where the chain was attached to the wall. I saw that the final link was a hook. She could have walked out of that cell by simply unhooking the chain from the wall.

Why do we find it difficult to change?

Sometimes a change of attitude can be effected by a simple

revelation of what needs to be done. It may be possible to "unhook the chain" and walk free by ourselves in response to God's revealed truth. But it isn't always as easy as that. For some, change takes a longer time and is hard; we find resistance within ourselves. Sometimes there are factors that militate against change in our lives, no matter how great our desire for change may be when we see what is needed.

Most psychiatrists and counsellors would agree that our basic needs are love, security and significance. (I would add "adventure" and "challenge" to the list!) Many of us have experienced damage in our lives, which hinders our ability to receive and trust those who would bring love and security into our lives, including God himself.

If change does not take place, this attitude of self-protectiveness can affect us right through our lives – especially during the "marriage" and "mothering" seasons, as we shall see later in the book.

Life is seasonal

The seasons of our life are not always as clearly defined and predictable as the seasons of the year. For some, singleness is a season which can last a lifetime. For others, it is a season to which they return when divorce or bereavement changes their situation. Some women, who had planned when they married to move into the mothering season, find their plans frustrated as, month after month, they are unable to conceive in spite of their longing for a baby. There are those who find themselves unexpectedly pregnant again after they had considered their family to be complete; for them, the mothering season is extended, and if this happens around the menopause they may find themselves mothering teens and toddlers at the same time. Some who embark on late motherhood after a fulfilling career find that a screaming baby is a greater challenge to them than a group of office trainees or a class of school leavers.

The sleepless nights of the baby and toddler years, the sunshine and storms of the teenager-mothering season, the bittersweet pain of the "empty nest", the need to care for elderly parents, the joyful amazement of grandmotherhood, the slow realization of ageing – all these new seasons of life require us to embrace them and adapt to them as women of God. When we are unable to adapt, our growth in God is slowed down or even halted. The depressed single woman who feels that her life is wasted without a partner, the mother who, for financial reasons, cannot stay at home with her baby and who returns to work reluctantly and bitterly, the woman who is still in deep sorrow two years after her children have left home, the divorced wife who is still full of bitterness toward her ex-husband several years later – these are all examples of women who have failed to adapt to the new season in their lives.

Adapting isn't easy

Adapting to a new season of life is not always easy, as I know from my own experience. During the years of my life I have faced many new situations – marriage at the age of 21, first baby at the age of 22, becoming a pastor's wife at the same time as my fourth (very unexpected) pregnancy at the age of 30, moving house and church several times, a husband who was frequently away from home on ministry trips, a serious operation, a long period of depression, church problems, marriage difficulties, problem teenagers (one of whom was anorexic for several years), a period of time when my husband was unemployed, and the break-up of my son's marriage.

There has been a constant need to adapt my attitudes to my current "season", and there have been times of great pain and turmoil. But God has given me much joy, too. His love, and the power and truth of his word, have helped me adapt to the difficult situations which he has allowed to come into my life. The body of Christ, made up of brothers and sisters who love him and who love me, has cared for me and strengthened me, and is still doing so. This book has come into being as I have shared my life with my sisters in Christ who are going through changes in their own lives. Some of them are still struggling with painful situations; some have experienced changes which rocked their lives. But for many of them, God's power has enabled them to accept and adapt to their "changing seasons" and to trust him as they walk in their new direction.

Some attitudes are reactive

My friend Joyce refuses to change her furniture around. Her bedroom and living-room must always look the same as they did when she first arranged them, however many house-moves she makes. Joyce's mother died when she was seven, and ever since then Joyce has wanted the security and assurance of things which remain exactly the same.

When we have been deeply hurt, or abused, we feel vulnerable. We may want to keep people at a distance, fearing closeness in case we are hurt again. When our children were young my husband Richard would never allow us to have any kind of argument (even a slight disagreement!) in front of them. His early childhood had been a time of constant, angry fighting between his parents before their marriage finally broke up when he was nine years old. He did not want our children hearing any quarrelling at all between their parents. This rather backfired years later, when one of our daughters, newly married, told us that when she and Martin, her husband, had had an argument shortly after their wedding, Leigh was convinced that they were heading for the divorce court, so unused was she to hearing domestic disagreement. (Lest anyone should think we achieved constant marital harmony, I assure you that we had our moments, in private!)

Clearly, some of our attitudes spring from specific life events which have caused us pain, and the result of our pain is a desire for self-protection. But we are influenced more than we realize by secular mind-frames and attitudes. Three of the most powerful of these are materialism, feminism and negativism; these attitudes, in various forms, can affect our lives through every "season". We will look at these "learned" attitudes in greater detail.

Materialism

A materialistic attitude and a desire for "things" can become apparent at any season of our life. It can strike when we receive a promotion at work and find we have more money available, when we return to work after raising a family, when we move to better or larger accommodation, when we inherit a legacy, when we are under stress. Or it can creep into our life when Jesus is not at the centre, or when we are not experiencing his love and closeness. We don't have to have money to be materialistic; in fact, the less money we have, the more our materialism will be linked to jealousy and covetousness, to say nothing of resentment! (Yes, we're talking about Christians – I know, I've been there!)

A materialistic mind-set can affect us because of a situation

in our life. Richard and I have recently moved into a new
house – new to us but actually a very decrepit Victorian ter-
raced cottage. We were able to buy the house cheaply because
of its terrible condition but then we had to set about making
it habitable. Builders did the basic repairs and renovations;
then we had to decorate the whole house. Thanks to the help
and hard work of our church family we finished in a few
weeks. I had chosen all the colours for the rooms; I enjoyed
decorating from scratch, without having to adapt to someone
else's choice of wallpaper and carpets.

We needed a new kitchen table and chairs. Then we needed
a new dresser, as there was no cupboard for kitchen equipment and spare china. We needed new wardrobes, as these
had been built-in where we had lived previously. We needed
new carpets in every room. We needed new bedlinen to match
the new bedroom décor. We needed new curtains; we needed
a new hall table, new lamps. The list was endless! I was buying magazines every month: *House Beautiful* and *Homes and
Ideas* really had me fired up.

Then came the day when the extra mortgage money we
had earmarked for "repairs and furnishings" was finished. I
had wonderful plans, and the sudden realization that there
was no more money proved a real shock to my system. I
couldn't think how we were going to manage without all the
other items on my "want" list. But as I looked at the list, I
realized that it was just that – a *want* list. All the real needs
had been supplied; the things I wanted now were definitely
cosmetic! As I looked into my heart, I recognized that I had
become addicted to "home furnishings". There was nothing
wrong in wanting an attractive home, and we were planning
to use it for the Lord, but I realized that for months my

thoughts and my commitment had been centred on furnishing and beautifying bricks and mortar. I had to backtrack and ask my Lord to take away the desire for "things". I had to make him and his love and grace the centre of my life again.

"My kids are going to have the best"

Many of us can remain free from materialistic attitudes until we have children. Then, somehow, the need is there to demonstrate that our offspring deserve the best of everything, even if the best proves to be the most expensive. From baby and toddlerhood (when clothes have to be Osh Kosh or Baby Gap) to teenage trainer time (naturally Nike or Reebok), our children must be seen to be wearing the latest in fashionable consumer gear. It goes without saying that the said children (encouraged by constant media advertising) totally agree with this! They must also have a computer with all the latest games, to say nothing of the current "strip" of their favourite football team.

Sometimes this urge to supply our children with everything they could possibly desire comes from a deep need in our own hearts. Perhaps we had very little in material terms when we were children and we are determined that our own children will not lack in the same way. If we experienced rejection as children because of our lack of clothes and possessions, we may feel absolutely determined that our children will not suffer similar rejection. So we make sure our children have the best. I know parents who will go into debt at Christmas and birthdays rather than deny their children something they want.

Parents who have suffered rejection themselves and who have never experienced God's healing in this area, may be fearful of saying "No" to their child for two reasons. They are afraid the child will feel rejected if he cannot have what he wants, and they are afraid that the child will reject them if they do not give him what he wants. These mistaken attitudes need to be confronted. Our love for our children is a powerful and strong emotion; we will do things for them that we would do for no one else. Yet we will be doing our children the greatest service if we will face our wrong attitudes, seek help and healing and begin to relate to our children without fear of rejection by them and without the urge to give them everything they want. The power of God's Holy Spirit can change our hearts in this area, and we can be free from destructive materialistic attitudes. Our own freedom will mean that our children, too, will be free from the harmful influence of these attitudes as they grow to adulthood.

Antidotes to materialism

As we have seen, materialism is often linked with jealousy, insecurity and discontent. The greater our understanding of who Jesus is, and of the totality of his claim upon our lives, the less likely are we to be gripped by these attitudes. How real is Jesus to you?

Last year Richard and I stayed in Prague, the beautiful capital city of the Czech Republic. One afternoon we visited the Catholic Church of Our Lady Victorious, where a waxwork model of Jesus as a little boy, known as the Holy Infant of Prague, is revered and honoured. A large team of nuns is responsible for making beautiful robes and vestments to adorn it. People were coming into the church to pray before the Holy Infant. I felt sad as I looked at the decorative but powerless effigy. Nowhere in the Bible do we read of Jesus performing miracles and receiving veneration as an infant of three or four years old. The real Jesus is not a child, any more than he is a baby in a manger – which is how he is pictured by the many who only think of him in December as part of Christmas. The real Jesus is alive, resurrected from the dead, seated at the right hand of the Father in heaven, yet gloriously present with those who have received salvation through his death on the cross.

Do you enjoy the love and presence of Jesus? Are you living in his mercy and grace? He is real. He is coming back again. This is not the only life. Grasping these realities will deliver us from materialism and prevent us wasting our affections on material objects and treasures which do not meet our deepest needs, though they may temporarily mask those needs.

If you can readily enjoy material realities but struggle to experience God's love, perhaps there have been hurts which have damaged you in the past. If you have only been loved conditionally, unconditional love may be more than you can handle. If you have been rejected by those who should have given you acceptance and loving care, you may have built a shell around yourself in order to guard against further hurt. But the shell which protects you from hurt will also prevent you from receiving the love and healing you need. There is a risk in becoming vulnerable, but taking that risk will bring you into a real relationship with a Saviour who gave his life so that you can know his personal and unconditional love filling your life. This, more than anything, will deliver you from materialistic attitudes.

Feminism

The secular mind-frame of feminism can also influence our attitudes. Men have treated women in terrible ways down the centuries. Napoleon Bonaparte, speaking for men, said, "Nature intended women to be our slaves . . . they are our property; we are not theirs. They belong to us, just as a tree that bears fruit belongs to a gardener. What a mad idea to demand equality for women! Women are nothing but machines for producing children." In the early years of the 20th century Pierre de Coubertin, founder of the modern Olympics, was unbelievably heard to remark, "Women have but one task, that of the role of crowning the victor with garlands." (Sally Gunnell and Denise Lewis, please note!)

The reaction of women against this kind of arrogant chauvinism became increasingly strong through the 20th century, matched by a determination to achieve everything men can achieve. Many books have been written about the rise of feminism in Britain and the heroic deeds of Emmeline Pankhurst and her daughters, who suffered imprisonment and loss of reputation to gain the vote for women. Two world wars and the invention of the contraceptive pill have helped to give women independence and opportunities which were once impossible dreams. Today's women in the Western world have the freedom to do and be whatever they want in almost every sphere. Yet still the "battle" for equality continues, and we find our blood pressure rising when we hear of issues and situations where women are suffering – whether in Islamic countries where their lives are rigidly controlled, in China where many girl babies are drowned at birth, stuffed into rubbish bins or suffocated (due to the one-child-one-family policy and the fact that families want sons) or here in the West where discrimination in the workplace as well as physical or emotional abuse in the home can be happening all around us.

In the ordinary, everyday events of our lives, women can frequently find themselves patronized by men, or taken advantage of, in situations where men put them down. We all know about the garage mechanics who think a woman does not know one end of a car from another, and many of us have experienced the humiliation of knowing that we are receiving less pay than a man doing a similar job. The recognition of these injustices can produce strongly militant feminist attitudes within us. But are these the right attitudes for Christian women? Are they pleasing to God? Can such attitudes create more problems in our emotional and spiritual life than the situations which caused them?

Feminist attitudes affect relationships

Though we may not all call ourselves feminists, Christian women can be deeply affected by this kind of attitude. During my years as a pastor's wife I have met many married women who have learned to despise their husbands. In most cases this has not been admitted but has been very evident in their relationship. Some of them came into marriage with unreal expectations, imagining that a Christian husband would solve all their problems and give them a new identity and self-image, as well as a wonderful life for ever after! Any woman coming into marriage with this attitude will realize very shortly after the wedding that no man is capable of doing this, and that, far from eliminating hers, a man actually brings his own needs and insecurities into the marriage. A woman who has looked for a strong husband upon whom she can lean and who will take responsibility in the home and in their relationship may be sadly disappointed when her husband is so laid-back that he leaves most of the family decisions to her. If he fails to take any spiritual lead in the marriage and does not pray with her or have any fellowship with her in the things of God, her disappointment will be compounded. From being disappointed it is a short step to despising his ineptitude, and then to becoming cynical and antagonistic towards men in general. Few men are likely to change when they live with a partner who views them in this way.

We have an enemy who wants us to be taken up with the war against men *instead of the war against sin*. If we make men our "number one enemy" we will waste an enormous amount of time and effort fighting a war which is not our war to fight. We want to stand for righteousness and justice, but making war on men is not the way to achieve that.

Antidotes to feminism

Feminists have a slogan about marriage: "When two are made one, the important question is, 'Which One?'" The implication here is that the man is likely to be the one who dominates the marriage and imposes his will upon the woman – and that this can only be bad. How does this mesh with scriptures like Ephesians 5:22: "the husband is the head of the wife", and 1 Peter 3:1: "Wives . . . be submissive to your husbands"? These verses would seem to underline the fact that men will dominate and Christian women must put up with it! Is this really what the Bible is teaching? If we look at the Scriptures through feminist eyes we will fail to see the truth that God gave authority to men for the protection and security of women, not as a threat to their security and their rights; godly male leadership is the biblical pattern. Because men have abused their position, women have been forced to fight for their rights and sometimes even for their own safety and that of their children.

If you are living with feminist attitudes and behaviour which are "learned" (from your mother? your daughter? your friends? the media?) you may need to take a step back from these attitudes and ask the Holy Spirit to show you truth and to "renew your mind", so that you may have a biblical view of men.

A "servant heart"

There is within all of us (men as well as women) a tendency to fight for our "rights", but sometimes members of the female sex throw the baby out with the bath-water. We are so determined not to be dominated by any man that we remove ourselves from the possibility of benefiting from a secure, Christ-like male leadership, whether it is coming from a husband or a church leader. Because we will not be "told what to do" by a man, we forget the desire of Jesus that his followers should have servant hearts. If we look at scriptures such as Matthew 20:28: "The Son of Man did not come to be served, but to serve", Galatians 5:13: "You . . . were called to be free. But do not use your freedom to indulge the sinful nature; rather serve one another in love" and 1 Peter 4:10: "Each one should use whatever gift he has received to serve others", the issue becomes one of obedience. Galatians 2:20 tells me that "I have been crucified with Christ and I no longer live, but Christ lives in me."

Feminist attitudes do not sit easily with a servant heart and a recognition that Jesus wants to live his life through us. This is especially so if we have a demanding career which may have developed aggressive traits within us; these very traits may have enabled us to climb promotion ladders in competition with men. Coming home in the evening to a husband who is to be our "head" is not an easy thing to do – except that Christian husbands are also to have "servant hearts" and we are to "submit to one another out of reverence for Christ" (Ephesians 5:21).

A forgiving heart

Some women have been deeply damaged by men. My friend Emily met Tom, her Christian husband, at a Bible college evening course. They married and started a family; Emily gave up her nursing career. After their first baby arrived, Tom became cold, closed and secretive toward Emily, and she discovered that he had no interest in being a caring or loving father to either of their first two children. Emily became deeply disappointed in her marriage and felt that something was seriously wrong; she longed for him to change.

When she was pregnant with their third child, Tom attended a Christian conference as a delegate from their church. Emily spent the three conference days fasting and praying at home, asking God to reveal the problem in their relationship. Tom returned home at the end of the third conference day. "I need to talk to you," he said to Emily as he walked through the door. He told her that God had met with him at the conference, and he confessed to her that during the seven years of their marriage he had been involved in homosexual relationships. He recognized the sin of this and prayed for God's forgiveness; he also asked his wife to forgive him for the damage he had caused to their marriage. Emily believed that now, with God's help, they could have a normal marriage and family life. For a time this seemed to be happening, and Tom made plans to leave his secular job and train for the ministry.

The family moved house in order for him to attend college. At this point Emily discovered that he had had an affair with a young girl at their church who had babysat for them. This betrayal shattered her and was harder to forgive than the homosexual episodes. He professed great sorrow and promised that it would not happen again; as far as Emily knows it did not. But during his college training he again became involved in the gay lifestyle, and for his wife the nightmare continued. In due course, the college authorities were informed of his sexual activities by some of Tom's fellow students. He was told that because of his behaviour he could not be ordained in his denomination, so when his training ended he applied for a position as manager of a community centre run by the denomination.

Eventually, Tom's ordination went ahead with another denomination which was prepared to overlook his past, and he began leading a church. Emily supported him; he had vowed to her after leaving college that he would never again become involved in gay sex. He kept that promise: his next affair was with a woman. One night he told Emily and his family that he had been in a relationship for six months and that he was leaving them to join his lover. He left that same evening. His younger daughter was devastated; his elder daughter furiously angry. His son had left home and become involved in the drug scene, deeply affected by the lack of fathering and normal family life.

After he had left, Emily realized that she would have to

divorce him; his activities and deception had finally ended her hopes of a change in their situation. The church members, in spite of their shock and disappointment at the behaviour of their pastor, were helpful and supportive. Emily and the children were allowed to remain in the church house until she could arrange accommodation for them all. She was able eventually to train as a history teacher, and life became more bearable for her after her disappointing marriage finally came to an end. She made a home for her children, feeling that at last the nightmare was behind her. But more was to come: Emma, her elder daughter, confessed to Emily one day that Tom had sexually abused her on a regular basis since she was a little girl. She had spoken to her younger sister and discovered that she, too, had been abused. Emily felt sick at these disclosures but recognized that the police and social services would have to become involved. Tom is now in prison.

Emily has been single now for five years. She would love to marry again but at the moment her children need her committed attention. She has never forgotten hearing her eldest daughter say, "From the time I was eleven I accepted that I no longer had a father." She acknowledges the pain they have suffered. I asked Emily how she has coped with this "forgiveness marathon". It has been hard, especially as she sees the long-term effect of his behaviour on the children. "I have forgiven him," she said. "It's very hard sometimes, when I remember what he has done. But I know I must forgive – if I don't, I will become bitter and I don't want that. I know that bitterness would damage me, and I've got to stay healthy for the children." She is right; the bitterness of unforgiveness can damage a person emotionally, and even physically, even more than the original unforgiven injury. I asked Emily if the events of her life had hardened her attitude towards men. "No," she said. "What happened to me hasn't turned me against men, because I have seen Christian marriages that are good. But when there is sin in a man's life, there will be problems in his marriage."

Emily's determination to maintain a forgiving heart toward Tom, and to trust God for her own and her children's future, has made her strong. She knows that God heard her cry for help and was with her through those terrible years. She believes God has given her a promise from Psalm 90 and that he will fulfil it in her life: "Make us glad for as many days as you have afflicted us, for as many years as we have seen trouble. May your deeds be shown to your servants, your splendour to their children. May the favour of the Lord our God rest upon us" (Psalm 90:15–17).

God wants strong women. But unforgiving, feminist attitudes do not produce strength; they hinder growth and fruit in a woman's life. Feminism often justifies its hard attitudes as "righteous indignation" over the behaviour of men. But "righteous indignation" is often a euphemism for "rationalized unforgiveness". Is this something you need to consider in your own life? The death of Jesus on the cross made it possible for us to be forgiven; his death also enables us to show mercy and forgiveness to others and to ourselves. This is not just a feminist issue; it is a vital principle.

The parable of the unmerciful servant in Matthew 18 shows clearly that God's forgiveness toward us must result in our forgiveness of those who have wronged us. If we have been hurt and damaged, we may feel very vulnerable and fearful of trusting people or risking new relationships. We may fear that if we forgive, we will somehow be minimizing the wrong done to us. But to extend forgiveness is not to rewrite the story, eliminate the pain or remove the memories. It is to create a doorway that will lead us through to wholeness and healing; it is God's appointed way of moving us on from the hurt we have suffered. To forgive others, and to be able to forgive ourselves, is vital if we are to move on in our lives, whether the hurt has been caused by abusive men or other factors or people. If we have "buried" the hurt and resumed normal life, we will have to do some "exhuming" in order to face our need to forgive. Forgiving is an act of our will. Jesus forgave those who were nailing him to the cross; only his power can enable us to do the same, and only his power and love can heal the hurt and damage.

Negativism

Some people see a glass as half full, some see it as half empty. A positive and optimistic person (seeing her glass as half full!) will cope more easily in a difficult situation.

Anyone who has read *Twopence to Cross the Mersey*, the amazing autobiography of Helen Forrester, will have marvelled at her resilience and positive determination in the face of disaster. Her wealthy father lost all his money and declared himself bankrupt when Helen was twelve years old. She was the eldest of six children, the youngest a tiny baby, when the family had to leave their beautiful house in Hoylake to live in slum lodgings in Liverpool during the years of the depression following the first world war. All they took with them were the clothes they were wearing. Helen was kept home from school to look after the younger children while her mother, who had been emotionally devastated by the events that had overtaken the family, sought any work she could get. Their abject poverty and inability to cope with life makes tragic reading. But Helen was determined to fight her way out of the trap in which she found herself, and eventually persuaded her discouraged and uncaring parents to allow her to attend evening classes, the first step back to completing her education. Through all the terrible problems and disappointments in her life, she stayed focused on this one aim and showed enormous qualities of survival and adaptability. Helen Forrester was determined to see her glass as being half full; she remained positive in spite of her dreadful situation and surroundings.

Negativism seems to be a peculiarly British complaint. Perhaps this is due to all the conversation about our unpredictable weather! Negativism can sap our energy and make our life colourless and tiring. But negativism in the life of a Christian woman can also be a severe hindrance to her growth and fulfilment. It is a "way of seeing" which can produce anxiety, discontent, cynicism and despair. If we hold on to negative attitudes our vision will become distorted and we will move away from faith and trust in our God and thanksgiving for his salvation and grace. We will fail to appreciate his provision and planning for our lives.

We read in Exodus about the wanderings of the Israelites in the wilderness after their miraculous passage through the Red Sea. God supplied their need for food with manna and quail, and guided them by a pillar of cloud by day and a pillar of fire by night. During this 40-year time span, according to Deuteronomy 8, God preserved their clothes so that they never deteriorated. (Eat your heart out, Marks and Spencer!) In spite of all this loving provision, the Israelites grumbled and complained, wanted to go back to their slavery in Egypt, and worshipped an idol when Moses, their leader, was absent from the camp. Because of their resentment and grumbling, God would not let them enter the promised land. When that generation had all died, God took the next generation into the land. We can easily be tempted to become negative in our thinking if we are living in a difficult situation. But if we continually grumble and complain, we will find that negative attitudes begin to dominate our life and prevent us entering into the goodness of God's promises, as surely as the grumbling of the Israelites lost them their opportunity to enter the promised land.

What causes negative thinking?

If we have a negative parent or parents, we may have inherited a tendency to think negatively. I had a very anxious mother, who always anticipated the worst scenario in any situation. She was also a very cynical person. When I became a Christian, and especially as I grew older, these were the two areas where I had to fight many battles for the renewing of my mind. Many of my friends admit to similar battles in areas where their parents (especially their mothers) were affected by negative attitudes. An inherited tendency may grow in our lives almost unconsciously; we are often unaware that we are reflecting parental attitudes. If we do not deal with these attitudes in our own lives, we will pass them on to our children, just as they have been passed on to us.

If we spend time with friends who are negative people, their attitudes will rub off on us. Presumably the Israelites in the wilderness were not all grumbling and complaining from the beginning. Probably a few discontented grumblers affected the others until it became so bad that God had to deal severely with the whole nation. People who allow negative attitudes to govern their lives will draw you into the same attitudes if you spend a lot of time in their company.

Believing the lies of Satan will also lead us into negative thinking. Last week I was talking to my friend Edwina, who is also my dentist. (I love her dearly, except when she has her nasty instruments in my mouth.) She told me that she had discovered recently that she had been cheated by Satan and robbed of much of her inheritance of peace and joy in God. Edwina has had to be the family breadwinner for the past two years, and one of her sons has a serious and chronic illness. She found herself deeply resenting all of this, frequently telling God and others how awful her situation was. But recently she has recognized the truth that God is sovereign over her life and that the negative attitude she has been carrying is Satan's lie to convince her otherwise. The Bible tells us, in the words of Jesus, that Satan is a liar (John 8:44) and that he is a thief whose purpose is to steal, kill and destroy.

Edwina saw that her attitude of negativism had developed as a result of believing Satan's lies about her life. She told me that she had had to confess this as sin and repent before God. Then she began to exercise faith in God's word. She would quote scriptures aloud, consciously and deliberately receiving the truth of the words into her heart. Some scriptures became particularly precious to her as she built a "storehouse" of truth into her inner being. She put doubts and negative attitudes away from her, replacing them with trust in the love and sufficiency of God and his personal care of her. The more she spoke out truth and believed it, the more God confirmed it in her heart. His peace and joy have taken the place of her previous negative attitude.

She has begun to see changes in her circumstances as she

has affirmed her faith in the word of God. Elliot, her son, who has a serious kidney disease, is now well enough to be in full-time school – and is also playing for the school rugby team! His blood tests show that he still has the kidney problem but God is honouring Edwina's faith in his word which says that his power is able to heal sickness and disease. One positive dentist!

A "storehouse of truth" can be our most powerful weapon in the battle to change our attitudes and mind-sets to those which God wants for us. The positive truth of God is the greatest "antidote" to negative thinking. If we receive and stand firm in the reliable promises of the Scriptures we can be "made new in the attitude of [our] minds" (Ephesians 4:23). But to stand firm in the truth we have to know it and believe it, as Edwina discovered. We will look at this more closely in the next chapter.

Recognizing negativism

Recognizing and acknowledging negative attitudes in our lives is the first step towards challenging them. Negativism frequently goes under the name "realism" in our vocabulary. We look at the state of the world and the church and convince ourselves that those who believe God is in control and is working out his purposes are misguided optimists. Negativism also narrows our viewpoint – so check your horizons! Negative attitudes cause us to be parochial and insular, concerned only about our own situations; we fail to look outward to embrace the lives and needs of other people or nations. Have you moved on and grown in your faith and your emotional life this past year? Negativism does not move on; it is going nowhere. If you stay with this way of thinking, you will remain static. Negative people don't enjoy life much; they are too aware of the problems, both actual and potential, of their faith, their families and relationships, their work and the fate of the nation. Their hormones ensure that once a month everything takes a turn for the worse! How can we, as Christian women, combat negativism when we recognize it in our lives?

Antidotes to negativism

We need to take our stand on the truth of God. Negative attitudes come from believing Satan's lies, as we saw earlier. Focusing on truth enables us to jettison the lies which Satan loves to infiltrate into our lives. The "realism" lie is far from real! Yes, we do live in a sad and broken world and many of us suffer, but the truth is that in Jesus we have hope; he is a Saviour who can mend the broken lives of all who give themselves to him. He is the greatest reality; the more we trust him and allow his truth to be the foundation for our life, the more we will see the world and our situation through his eyes. He has a positive perspective!

Believing truth, as Edwina experienced, changes the way we understand the situations of our life, and our anticipation of the outcome. I became diabetic four years ago, and soon after the diagnosis, some well-meaning people sent me a paper telling me about all the possibilities I was to anticipate: kidney disease, heart problems, increased likelihood of a stroke, eye damage possibly leading to blindness, and amputation of various extremities due to gangrene! The paper also informed me that diabetes is the third leading cause of death by disease in the Western world, after heart disease and cancer. My heart sank as I put the paper down. I went to make a cup of coffee and thought about what I had read – it seemed like a death sentence. Then my faith began to rise as I thought about the fact that it is Jesus who holds the keys of death (Revelation 1:18), and I am in *his* hands. *He* is Lord of my life, and I am certainly not going to let diabetes take his place, nor am I going to spend time worrying about complications which may or may not arise in the future. I take on board what Jesus says in chapter six of Matthew's gospel, that worrying will not add a single hour to my life and that I am to live a day at a time, seeking *his* kingdom above everything else. I'm doing all the right medical things, but the outcome is in his hands, and I am content to leave it there. I still have the horrific prognosis paper but I don't read it or think about it. God's truth is my firm foundation; that is our greatest weapon against negative thinking.

Don't be critical of others

Negativism produces within us a critical, judgmental attitude toward others; it also harms our own self-image. A critical attitude does not make for easy or joyful relationships in the family, the workplace or the church, particularly as those who are judgmental of others are usually on the alert for the slightest criticism of themselves. This attitude grieves the Holy Spirit, who wants to produce his fruit of love, joy, peace, patience, kindness, goodness, faithfulness, gentleness and self-control in our lives (Galatians 5:22–23). If you recognize negative and critical attitudes in yourself, it's time to repent and ask God for his forgiveness and cleansing. Then ask Jesus to help you see people through his eyes of love and compassion. Read through the gospels and see how Jesus related to people – he was a very positive person, and he can put his attitudes within you if you are willing for change. This won't be instantaneous, but if you take one day at a time, with the Holy Spirit's help it can happen!

Catherine Marshall describes in her book *A Closer Walk* (Hodder & Stoughton, 1987), how God convicted her of the sin of being critical and judgmental towards people and situations. God spoke very clearly to her from Matthew 7:1–2: "Do not judge, or you too will be judged. For in the same way you judge others, you will be judged, and with the measure you use, it will be measured to you." She felt that God was telling her to go on a "fast" from criticism for one whole day. For the first part of the day, Catherine felt as if she had been "wiped out" as a person; she was not free to offer any of her witty insights on any subject, even at a family lunch. She realized how judgmental her opinions usually were, as she listened to the others at the table expressing their thoughts while remaining silent herself. "Several topics came up," she writes, "on which I had definite opinions. Barbed comments on the tip of my tongue about certain world leaders were suppressed. In our talkative family no one seemed to notice. Bemused, I realized that my comments were not missed. The federal government, the judicial system and the institutional church could apparently get along fine without my penetrating observations!"

In the afternoon, Catherine spent time praying and writing. God gave her understanding and revelation about a matter she had been praying over for a long time; when she came later in the afternoon to her writing project she found that her ideas began to flow in a way she had not experienced for years. "Now it was apparent what the Lord wanted me to see," she writes. "My critical nature had not corrected a single one of the multitudinous things I had found fault with. What it *had* done was to stifle my own creativity – in prayer, in relationships, perhaps even in writing – ideas that he wanted to give me." And that was after one day! Would a similar day's "fast" help you to begin changing negative and critical attitudes?

More antidotes to negativism

Spend time deliberately giving thanks to God – this is a positive way to build your faith. A thankful heart which appreciates God's grace and love will not be thinking negatively. Philippians 4:6–7 is a wonderful scripture for anxious, negative people. Write it on a card and put it over your sink (or dishwasher, or computer!). Receive this truth, meditate on it, trust it! "Do not be anxious about anything, but in everything, by prayer and petition, *with thanksgiving*, present your requests to God. And the peace of God, which transcends all understanding, will guard your hearts and your minds in Christ Jesus." I have proved the truth of this many times in all sorts of situations, from financial struggles to problem teenagers – and it is powerful!

Spend time with "positive" friends. If you tend to be a negative person, other negative people will feed your attitude and you will become even more negative and discouraged. Ask God to give you friends who love him and who will bless you, build you up and help you to change.

Having looked at these destructive, growth-preventing attitudes, and seen some positive antidotes to them, we will go on to look, in the next chapter, at two vitally important factors which will constantly work to bring our hearts into line with God's desire to conform us to the likeness of Jesus and enable us to live in our present "season of life" with attitudes which honour God and lead to growth and maturity. These are God's sovereignty and God's grace. We will also take a look at the other resources that God has made available to us.

To consider: Do you recognize any of these attitudes in your present "season" of life? If so, which "antidotes" do you need to apply?

CHAPTER TWO

ATTITUDE-CHANGERS

We have seen in chapter 1 that only when we believe and receive truth does it become effective in our lives, changing our attitudes and our behaviour. The wonderful twin truths of God's sovereignty and God's grace can be powerful factors in helping us to be "conformed to the likeness of his Son" (Romans 8:29). The power of God's word and his Holy Spirit, and the fellowship of the family of God, will become a firm foundation in our lives enabling us to take the risk of reaching toward change.

The certainty of God's sovereignty

The sovereignty of God is the doctrine which is challenged more than any other. The favourite comment of unbelievers, when confronted with the kind of event which shocked the civilized world on 11 September 2001 or with news of anything from war and suffering in the Balkans to starving street children in South America is, "How can you say there is a God? If there were, he would stop all this!"

As Christians who know the truth, we will also at times be tempted to say, "How can God be sovereign in *this* situation?" In every season of our lives this truth will be challenged. As a pastor's wife I have often listened to people who come to share their individual stories of abuse, incest, neglect and sheer cruelty. I have wept with people over the pain and rejection that has come from those who should have loved them. I have cried with single women who have lived for years with their longing for a partner. I have heard the heartache of Christian couples who have desperately desired children yet who have never achieved a pregnancy, and I have wept with those who have given birth to a disabled child whose needs are going to radically alter their life. Is God *really* sovereign over the individual lives of his children? Can we trust the truth of this?

I used to find it very wearing and difficult to plough through the genealogical lists in the Bible. I couldn't see that it mattered how old Arphaxad was when he begat Shelah! But one day God spoke to me about this; he showed me that each of these names indicated someone he knew personally. They were not just lists of unpronounceable names attached to unknown, boring people; they were the names of people he had chosen to work out his purposes on the earth. These lists of people were demonstrations of God's sovereignty. This gave me a different perspective. Becoming diabetic four years ago gave me a different perspective on chocolate! A new perspective enables us to have a new attitude. Have you understood and believed that God is sovereign?

Did God really choose me?

The most amazing, mysterious and powerful truth in the

Bible is the fact of God's sovereignty over our lives. I believe the Bible teaches that God planned my existence, my parentage, my sex, my nationality. He knew how long I would be single and who I would marry. He also planned that in my early teens I would recognize my need of him and experience his salvation. As I read Psalm 139 (which I do, frequently) I am overwhelmed by his close and personal sovereign love. Yet he also gives me free will. Only after I had given my life to him did I discover in John's gospel that I had not chosen him, but he had chosen me! Charles Spurgeon, one of the great preachers of the 19th century, explained this by comparing God's salvation to a huge archway over which are written the words, "whoever believes . . . shall not perish but have eternal life" (John 3:16). When we have "walked through" the archway, we look back and see that over the other side of it is written, "chosen in Christ before the creation of the world" (Ephesians 1:4).

Does he know what is happening to me?

I believe God also knew the suffering, pain and failure which would come into my life, and that this was part of the way he would shape my character and enable me to learn to trust his mercy and grace. Even our failures and mistakes are somehow woven into the plans of our loving God, who has total knowledge of our lives.

Trusting in God's sovereignty will bring security and a change of perspective into our lives, especially as we work to bring our attitudes in line with the season of life in which we are living. This is not a "fatalistic" way of looking at life but rather a recognition that our mighty God loves each one of us intimately and cares for each one of us personally.

Sometimes his dealings with us are a mystery. If we look at the Bible we shall see that this has been the case from the beginning of time. Daniel was delivered from the lions; Stephen was stoned to death. Peter was rescued from prison by an angel; John the Baptist was beheaded at the request of a dancing girl. Were these hit-or-miss happenings, or was God ordering the outcome of these people's life situations? Look at Daniel 3 – the story of the three men who were put into a blazing furnace because they would not worship the golden idol set up by the king, Nebuchadnezzar. Their attitude of trust in God's sovereignty over their lives shines out as the king tells them that if they do not worship the idol they will be burnt to death. They reply, "O Nebuchadnezzar, we do not need to defend ourselves before you in this matter. If we are thrown into the blazing furnace, the God we serve is able to save us from it, and he will rescue us from your hand, O king. *But even if he does not*, we want you to know, O king, that we will not serve your gods or worship the image of gold you have set up" (Daniel 3:16–18).

Shadrach, Meshach and Abednego had no doubt that God knew what was happening to them and that the outcome was in his purposes, whatever it meant for them. It was this knowledge that changed their perspective and enabled them to go into that terrifying situation with serenity. And they found, in the heat and the terror, that they could walk unharmed and that God walked in the furnace with them.

He is in control

The certainty that Jesus "walks through the fire" with us and that he works all things together for the good of those who love him (Romans 8:28) is a powerful factor in changing our attitudes. There will be disasters, pain and failure in our lives; there will be situations we wrestle with; there will be events we can neither understand nor cope with – but there will also be God's mercy and grace to depend on in our time of need, and the awareness that he is with us and that things are not "out of control". We do not see the whole picture; he does. We do not understand how pain and frustration can produce any good in our lives, but he knows us intimately and has a plan for us which involves changing us into his likeness. He is concerned about our character rather than our convenience!

We have a choice – we can resist, fight and refuse to learn from our frustrations and difficulties or we can trust God's sovereignty in our lives and receive his perspective as we live through the situation. The pain will still be there but we will know he is in it too, weeping with us over our sorrows, loving us as we suffer and knowing how he will shape and change us through what he allows to come into our lives. For, make no mistake, it is *God* who allows the events that cause pain and seeming disaster in our lives. Some Christians attribute all calamities to the work of Satan. But our lives are in the hands of our almighty God; Satan is a defeated foe, and he cannot affect our lives except with God's permission. Our circumstances are "Father-filtered", even the ones we cannot understand or handle.

Paul, the travelling apostle, suffered a great deal because he preached the gospel; he was beaten, shipwrecked and betrayed. We can read the catalogue of his hardships in 2 Corinthians 11. He was frequently imprisoned for his faith but out of his frequent prison sentences came the epistles to the Ephesians, the Philippians and the Colossians, as well as letters to Timothy and Philemon. Paul in prison meant the truth of God coming to us!

God knows the end from the beginning

Only God knows the whole picture. When we read the book
of Job, we understand from the very first chapter that God
knew exactly what was happening to his servant. Job's struggle to trust God through the assaults of Satan was a visual aid
for those around him and for us – but Job did not know that;
he had not heard the conversation between God and Satan
which we read about at the beginning of the book. Job's suffering and loss was terrible, culminating in the death of his ten
children. Finally his health left him, and his desolation was
complete. (Job's wife is a woman to admire; in spite of her
failure to trust God as Job did, we read in the last chapter of
the book that God restored to Job all that he had lost and that
he went on to have ten more children, presumably with the
same wife. . . .)

Some years ago I was part of a fortnightly drivers' rota taking my friend Eunice and her three-year-old son Tim to the
Royal Marsden Hospital, where Tim was receiving treatment
for leukaemia. At this hospital the large room where patients
waited to see their consultants was next to the blood-testing
area. Many of the leukaemia patients were toddlers. Every
time they visited the hospital they had to have blood taken for
testing, and for many of them this was a terrible ordeal; we
could hear their screams from where we sat in the waiting-
room. One little girl, Mandy, was particularly terrified – she
also had a particularly strong pair of lungs. One day I was sitting in the waiting-room. Tim had gone with Eunice to see
his consultant. Mandy had been called for a blood test and we
heard the screams begin as her mother tried to calm and reas-

sure her. But it was no use: as the decibel level rose we all felt Mandy's pain.

At that point I heard the voice of God speak into my heart: *"All of you feel sympathy for Mandy. But the one who is suffering most is her mother. She is holding Mandy and watching her go through the pain. Mandy has no understanding of the reason why this is necessary; she just knows that it is hurting her a lot and she wants her mother to stop it happening. But her mother sees the whole picture and knows that this is an important part of the treatment for this illness. She suffers with Mandy, identifies with her pain, but is aware that the future outcome depends on what is happening now. I love my children with a Father's love and I identify with them when they suffer, just as Mandy's mother identifies with her. And I know the whole picture; I know what I am doing in the lives of each one of my people."*

Mandy's blood test ended, Eunice and Tim emerged from the consulting room and we drove home. A year later Tim's treatment finished, apart from regular check-ups and medication. He is now a strong and vigorous young man, and probably never gives much thought to his lengthy treatment at "The Marsden". But I will always remember the insight God gave me in that hospital waiting-room. Only God sees the whole picture.

Sometimes God allows us to see, with hindsight, what he has been doing. Louise, a close friend of mine, miscarried her first baby. I sat with her in the hospital through this painful time and, as I comforted her, found myself questioning God. How could this be happening? Louise wondered if somehow her own actions had put the baby at risk. Should she have left work immediately she became pregnant? Perhaps she should not have carried shopping or cleaned the floor. A couple of weeks later I returned to the hospital with her for a scan, to ensure that her womb was clear of any debris from the miscarriage which could cause problems later. The scan showed a completely empty womb, and the tears flowed afresh. We talked about God's sovereignty and about trusting when we don't understand. As Richard and I prayed for Louise and David, our hearts ached for them. For Louise it was especially hard, as her sister Rosanna was also pregnant; their babies had been due the same week. In the days that followed the miscarriage, Rosanna hardly dared to talk about her baby in front of Louise. But as the weeks passed, Louise and David recognized that God was sovereign, and that he understood their sadness and identified with them in it.

As Louise recovered, she found herself able to comfort a friend who had just suffered a miscarriage. They began to look to the future. Louise again became pregnant and this time there were no problems. Three months after Rosanna gave birth to Joel, Louise produced Daniel – a healthy eight-pounder who has brought enormous joy to his parents. When Daniel was about two, Louise told me she had been thinking about the baby she had lost. "I realize," she said, "that if the first baby had been born, we would never have had Daniel. I'm sure it would have been a lovely baby, but it wouldn't have been *him*, and we love him so much!" God had taken the unborn baby to himself and sent them the one he planned for them to look after. Davina, their next baby, arrived after a very difficult and uncertain pregnancy. Twice Louise nearly lost her, but she eventually arrived safely, unaware of all the stress her journey towards birth had caused. But God wanted her here; of that we are certain.

We don't always have our questions answered

God does not always give us the benefit of hindsight which enables us to say, "So *that's* what God was up to!" Sometimes we are left with what James Dobson calls "the awesome why". In his excellent book *When God Doesn't Make Sense* (Tyndale, 1997) James Dobson tells the story of his four close friends who were all killed when their small aircraft crashed in a remote canyon *en route* to Dallas. They had been with him the previous day and he had prayed with them for their safety on the journey home. These men were Christian husbands and fathers, active in their professional careers and in the kingdom of God. James Dobson, himself devastated by the death of his friends, spoke of the days following the tragic event: "I was asked by the four families to speak briefly at their funeral. The untimely deaths of such vibrant and deeply loved men seemed to scream for an explanation. Where was God in their passing? Why did he let this happen? Why would he take such godly men from their families and leave them reeling in grief and pain? There were no answers to these agonising questions, and I did not try to produce them. But I did say that God had not lost control of their lives and that he wanted us to trust him when nothing made sense."

If we cannot trust the truth that God is in control, we will never be able to "move on" from the seemingly catastrophic events which happen in our own lives. We will be going back in our minds continually to the events and the people which have caused us pain and confusion. There is a children's game which consists of a pole with a long piece of elastic attached to it. Fixed to the end of the elastic is a tennis ball. When the ball is hit, however far, it always bounces back on its elastic rope to the place where it started. Our minds can become like this; if we have been deeply hurt, we can dwell on the event for years afterwards, coming back to it again and again, replaying all that happened and remembering how badly we were treated. If we do not recognize God's sovereignty over our lives, even over the events which have damaged us, we will never be able to come to a place of forgiveness toward those involved; neither will we be able to move forward from that event into the rest of our life. We will be like the ball on the elastic, continually returning to the event in our thoughts and allowing it to affect our attitudes, our behaviour and our relationships. Perhaps our resentment has been against God himself, for the pain he has allowed to come into our life. If this is so, we need to repent and reaffirm our trust in his love and his sovereignty.

The reality of God's grace

There have been many attempts to define "grace", and perhaps the best one is "undeserved favour". I think of it as "recognition of riches" – God making real to us all that we have in him. Our understanding of grace depends on two things: how we see God, and how we see ourselves. If you see God as a stern and upright father who, having received you into his kingdom, now requires your absolute commitment and total obedience before you dare approach him in prayer, and if you see yourself as an insignificant person who has only just scraped into the kingdom of God and must make sure you do everything God expects of you in order to "make the grade" as a Christian, it is probable that you do not know much about God's grace.

In his book *From Orphans to Heirs* (published by BRF, 1999), Mark Stibbe says, "My image of God for the first few years of my Christian life was that he was a stern judge, not a loving Father. I was taught to fear God, but not to love him. The net result of this was that I started to live a life of legalism rather than a life of love. However hard I tried, I couldn't live up to God's standards. I functioned as a slave rather than as a son. The main reason was because of a deficient image of God." In this magnificent book, Mark Stibbe goes on to tell how he was brought into an understanding of "God's adopting grace" which changed his life.

The devil is a liar, as we saw earlier. One of the ways in which he seeks to weaken Christians is to convince us that we have to earn the right to be accepted by God. We know that our salvation was accomplished through the death of Jesus on the cross, yet somehow we feel that we have to contribute something as well: live righteously, keep the commandments, pray, witness, read the Bible. If we are doing these things we can afford to believe that God accepts us and loves us. When we fail in any of these areas, we immediately feel condemned. When we sin, Satan (who is called "the accuser" in the book of Revelation) will bring before us all our past sins and make us lose hope of ever being any different. Guilt, rather than grace, becomes the dominant factor in our experience. If this describes you, here are some things to consider.

The power of the cross

Look at the cross, where Jesus conquered Satan once and for all. The cross is the greatest demonstration of God's grace. The price is paid for your sin. God has already punished Jesus; he will not now punish you or reject you. He has forgiven you, covered you with the righteousness of Jesus, given you a new nature and made you his own. Romans 3:22–25 tells us that "this righteousness from God comes through faith in Jesus Christ to all who believe" and that we are "justified freely by his grace through the redemption that came by Christ Jesus. God presented him as a sacrifice of atonement, through faith in his blood."

The cross was not God's "plan B" – it was his purpose from the very beginning that the blood of his crucified Son should be the means of our salvation. The cross was the instrument of God's wrath toward Jesus and the instrument of his grace toward us. Jesus' death is totally sufficient to satisfy God's requirement for the punishment of our sin; there is nothing we can do to add to its efficacy. No performance, no great deed, no feat of law-keeping can make us any more beloved or accepted by God than we already are. If we should sin, we know that the blood of Jesus will cleanse us (1 John 2:1,2). His blood is powerful for all time, right through our lives. We don't have to write ourselves off as "failed Christians", but rather rejoice in God's forgiveness and love.

We belong to him

Having considered the cross, and God's grace in giving his Son to die for us, we can rest in the fact that we are his own children. We have four children – Amy, Leigh, Andy and Katie; from the moment they were born into our family they were ours. We brought them up, loved them, protected them, praised them and disciplined them. At times they were disobedient; at times they rebelled against us. But we never stopped loving them, and even when they were being rebellious and disobedient they never stopped being ours. It would have broken our hearts if any of them had felt they needed to earn the right to be called our children. They were part of our family because they had been born to us. Being naughty could not take them out of our family, any more than being good could give another child the right to join our family. We loved them (and still do!) because they were our children, God's gift to us.

God's grace and love toward his children is far greater than human parental love, however strong. If we feel God only loves us when we are being good, it may be because we have only known conditional love; we find it difficult to grasp the concept of God's unconditional love and grace. We are part of God's family because Jesus died for us and has given us eternal life. We can't earn his favour or his gifts; he gives them to us freely. 2 Timothy 1:9 says that the reason why God has saved us and called us to a holy life is "not because of anything we have done but because of his own purpose and grace".

Grace produces gratitude

Our response to the grace of God must be to leave condemnation and guilt behind us and find our identity in being a chosen, forgiven and loved child of God. The more we do this, the more we will experience his love and grace. We will recognize that God is *for* us, not against us (Romans 8:31) and we will want to live for him out of gratitude and thanksgiving, not out of compulsion and fear. The grace of God in our life will bring about change in our attitudes, especially toward other people. As his grace fills our hearts and brings forth thanksgiving, so grace will flow from us to others.

My friend Debbie is also my hairdresser, so I see her often. I have known her since she was at school; she was part of our young people's group at church. Debbie had become a Christian in her teens and grew in faith through the years in spite of difficult home circumstances. Later she married Phil, who had also been part of the youth group, and they had two lovely children. A few years ago Debbie drifted away from God. She didn't like the way some things were being dealt with at church, and she decided that friends who were not Christians were far more interesting. She turned her back on Jesus and his followers, and developed a busy social life away from church. My friend Marion and I decided to pray regularly and specifically for her. She is Marion's hairdresser too, so she came to our homes frequently, and we often talked to her about God's love for her and how much he wanted her back; but she took no notice.

One day Marion invited Debbie to go to a meeting with her. It was one of a series of celebration meetings where God was moving powerfully. She agreed to go to the meeting with Marion "just to get her off my back!", she said. During the meeting one of the leaders came to the front and said God was telling him that there were several backsliders in the congregation – those who had gone away from God. He asked any of them who wanted prayer to go to the back of the church after the meeting was over. To Marion's amazement, Debbie joined the group of people afterwards to receive prayer. She told me what happened to her when she went to bed later that night. "I'd gone to sleep," she said, "and about midnight I suddenly woke up. It was as if I was standing at the bottom of a hill. I looked up and saw Jesus standing at the top. I started to walk up the hill towards him, and as I walked up he came running down towards me. When he reached me, he put his arms round me, lifted me up and swung me round! He said to me *'It's so good to have you back!'*" No condemnation, just love. By now Debbie and I were both in tears as we rejoiced in the grace of God towards her. It took a long time to get my hair done that day! Debbie is still walking with God, and her rekindled love for him has led to a desire to serve him and to bless others.

Grace produces discipline

The grace of God is a far greater motivator than the compulsion of condemnation and striving. When we are enjoying God's riches, and his Spirit is enabling us to understand all he has done for us, we will *want* to please him; gratitude and thanksgiving will be in our hearts. We will have a desire to meet with the Lord, to get to know him, read his word and spend time with him. This will involve discipline. Discipline is very different from legalism! In a busy life we have to exercise discipline in order to have quality time with our husbands, our children or our friends. We want to spend time with them, and discipline is what makes it happen. Choices have to be made.

Discipline of life is a response to grace. We are not trying to earn God's love – we already have it in abundance. God is *for* us, so we want to be *for* him. We already have God's approval, so we will not be always seeking the approval of others or constantly trying to please people. This will make for peace in our hearts and lives. God's grace in our lives is the greatest incentive to a holy life (2 Timothy 1:9). We really do not want to sin against the one who loves us so much.

Don't walk backwards

Once we have understood and appreciated God's grace, we

need to keep walking in that understanding and appreciation. Paul the apostle wrote strongly to the Galatian church when he heard that they were moving away from their understanding of the grace of God into a place of observing the law again. He told them that they were sons, not slaves, and that the law could not justify anyone, nor make a person righteous in the sight of God. If we lose sight of God's grace we, too, will be tempted to go back to a position of trying to "keep the law" and failing. God wants to change us and he will do it by his grace. We do not have to sin; it is not the "natural" thing for a Christian to do. Indeed, Titus 2:11–12 tells us that it is God's grace which enables us "to say 'No' to ungodliness". He gives us his Holy Spirit (more about that later in the chapter) who enables us to co-operate with God in changing our attitudes and behaviour to make us like Jesus. We can choose to offer ourselves to God as those who have been "brought from death to life" (Romans 6:13). We can choose to "offer the parts of [our bodies] to him as instruments of righteousness." Verse 14 tells us that sin does not have to master us, because we are not under law, but under grace.

The truth of God's word

In Luke's gospel Jesus says that a "good man brings good things out of the good stored up in his heart . . . For out of the overflow of his heart his mouth speaks" (Luke 6:45). A "storehouse of truth" is something we need to have if we are to grow and change. God's word must be in our hearts, minds and memories if we are to learn his wisdom and live his way. His truth, applied by the Holy Spirit, will govern our behaviour and our attitudes. But in order for this to happen we have to read it, receive it and feed on it. This means programming into our lives times of fellowship with God to read the Bible and pray. Doing this may seem impossible if we have a very busy schedule, but it is the only way we will grow in the wisdom of God and in our knowledge of him.

I remember an occasion in my life a year or two ago when the Lord really got my attention over the matter of spending time with him. I was extremely busy, with hardly a spare minute; I was also extremely tired and found it impossible to read the Bible and pray last thing at night. Most mornings I didn't have time for prayer or Bible-reading, or if I did, it was short and hurried. I knew it wasn't a good situation, that my spiritual resources for other people and for myself were running dry, and that some of my attitudes were becoming hard. Suddenly it was summer holiday time, and our church, together with hundreds of others, travelled to attend the Stoneleigh Bible Week: a whole week to worship God, hear the ministry of excellent speakers and have fellowship with my brothers and sisters in the Lord on our church caravan and camping site. Wonderful! But deep down I knew that all I really wanted was to creep into our tent and spend the week sleeping.

One afternoon I was in the tent (not asleep, but actually reading my Bible) when God spoke clearly into my heart. He directed me to the book of Hosea in the Old Testament. Hosea was a prophet to whom God revealed the sadness of his heart over Israel's coldness and lack of love; so far away from God were his chosen people that they were actually worshipping idols. The last chapter of the book tells of God's longing for his people to return to him and the promises he will fulfil in their lives if they will do so. As I read this chapter I felt God stop me at verse 5, where he says, "I will be like the dew to Israel." I knew he wanted me to think about this. I visualized a dew-washed landscape in the early morning, trees and grass sparkling in the warming sun – beautiful. And then God said to me *"Sue, dew only falls on things which stay still!"* I was stunned; God had put his finger so accurately on the lack in my life. I wasn't worshipping idols, but I knew that there was no "stillness" in my life at that point, no quietness for God to let the "dew" of his presence descend on me.

As I read the verses which followed, I realized how much I needed that "dew" for spiritual health and growth. I made those scriptures personal; I knew that God was saying to me that when he came as the "dew" into my life he would cause my roots to grow deeper into him (verse 5), shoots would grow up and there would be fragrance as others were blessed by dwelling in my shade. I would blossom, flourish and be fruitful (verses 7 and 8). I knew that I wanted this, and I knew that in order to get it I would have to make changes. When we returned home from the Bible Week, I gave up my part-time job. This meant I had less money but more time to spend in God's presence. My roots went deep again into the foundation of his love and truth. I received nourishment and insights from him which blessed me and others. And although we had less money, we never lacked what we really needed.

The more we feed on God's word, the greater will be our access to the wisdom and power of God. Whether we are dating a boyfriend, taming a toddler, coping with teens or an ageing parent, making a difficult decision or dealing with a crisis, God's wisdom is our reliable source of help. If his word is hidden in our hearts (Psalm 119:11) and we are enjoying fellowship with him, we will hear the Holy Spirit speaking to us. There may not be an instant answer to our problem; we are not programmed robots, and God has given us common sense and the ability to work things out. But his word of truth will steady us and enable us to see a way forward – and if not, to trust him until we do.

Distinguishing good from evil

The Bible tells us that feeding on the "solid food" of truth will also train us "to distinguish good from evil" (Hebrews 5:14). This kind of godly wisdom is urgently needed in our present culture. In the first decade of the new millennium we are made sharply aware that much which is labelled "fun" could be more aptly labelled "filth". We can become desensitized to truth by the world around us, and if we feed our minds and spirits too much from other sources than the word of God we will find that the lines between "good and evil" will become blurred. If God's word governs your attitudes, there will be some television programmes you will not watch, some women's magazines you will not buy, some computer games your children will not have and some seemingly good ideas you will not adopt. The more you feed your mind and spirit on the truth and wisdom of God, the stronger your life's foundation will be. We have an enemy who will try to woo us away from the word of God. If Satan cannot stop us reading the Bible he will cause us to question it, especially if we are going through difficult times or are particularly aware of fears or inadequacies. (We will consider this more in the next section.)

We saw in the previous chapter that Satan is a liar. He is also a destroyer (1 Peter 5:8) and an accuser (Revelation 12:10). When we recognize his activity in our lives we can counter it with the truth of God's word, as Jesus did when Satan tempted him (Matthew 4:1–11). Sometimes Satan "masquerades as an angel of light" (2 Corinthians 11:14) but if our minds are saturated with the word of God we will be able to "distinguish good from evil" and resist him.

Read the Bible as God's word for *you*. It's tempting to feel that some of the Old Testament books can't really be relevant to a "new millennium woman"! But Paul the apostle writes, "Whatever things were written before were written for our learning, that we through the patience and comfort of the Scriptures might have hope" (Romans 15:4, AV). He also tells us that "all Scripture is God-breathed and is useful for teaching, rebuking, correcting and training in righteousness" (2 Timothy 3:16).

Finding time for God's word

It isn't easy to fit Bible-reading and prayer into busy lives. I've shared my own experience of needing to slow down and find time for God – and that was after all my children had grown up! If you have babies and/or toddlers it can be almost impossible to manage a regular time unless you can negotiate with your husband or a friend to give you a free chunk of time. My daughter Leigh works three days in the week and has a routine which enables her to have a good long time with God on her two free days. She doesn't feel under condemnation about the other days because she knows this is right for her and she can fit it in with her family and work commitments.

How should you read the Bible? Should you start at Genesis and work your way through to Revelation? What about Bible commentaries? Should you use Bible-reading notes? Well, this book is more of an Egon Ronay guide than a restaurant menu, so I am not going to give you the detail; there are many good books available to help you read the Scriptures. The important thing is that you *do* read! It's also good to learn to meditate on what you read. Stay with one passage of scripture for a week or two and extract every bit of "spiritual nourishment" from it. Ask the Holy Spirit to teach you its meaning. I once spent six months in the epistle to the Ephesians, reading it whenever I could (my four children were all young at the time!), learning the background, drinking it in, applying it to my life. The riches of that epistle are still with me many years later. I remember reading through the first chapter and underlining all the blessings I had "in Christ". I felt like a millionaire! I learned about the power which brought about the resurrection of Jesus and what that means for me; about Christian relationships, about spiritual warfare. It's still my favourite epistle!

The power of the Holy Spirit

I had been a Christian for many years before I heard much about the Holy Spirit. I knew that the Holy Spirit had been active in my life to bring me to faith in Jesus when I was a teenager, and I knew that the Holy Spirit now lived in me because I belonged to Christ (Romans 8:9). But although I attended a keen evangelical church, I was never taught about the baptism and gifts of the Holy Spirit. If the gifts were ever mentioned it was in the context of the life of the early church and the first apostles, not as anything which was relevant to the church today. I loved the Lord, I had been baptized, I was part of the Christian Union at school and attended church with my friends every Sunday. I was known as a Christian and I had a real desire to walk with God and to know him better.

As I grew up I was never tempted to date non-Christian boyfriends; the essential ingredient would have been missing! When I met and married Richard we wanted to live for the Lord and to bring up our children to know him. We attended keen churches wherever we lived, and the children went to Sunday school as a matter of course. Eight years after our marriage, when we were living in a Kent village, the course of my life changed abruptly. Within the same week I received confirmation of my fourth (totally unexpected) pregnancy, and Richard came home and told me he knew God was calling him into full-time pastoral ministry. Within six months we had moved to a busy area of south London where Richard, who had for several years been working with a missionary organization linked to the Army and the Royal Air Force, became the pastor of a thriving evangelical church. A few weeks after our move I gave birth to Katie and settled down to learn about life as a pastor's wife.

Something missing

We had been in the church for about four years when I began to feel more and more that my Christian experience was not enough for the life I was now expected to live. For the first couple of years I had been very busy with the new baby and the other three children. Nobody minded if I wasn't at the prayer meeting or if I missed a few Sunday services. The church had called Richard as its pastor; he was totally committed to the work there and I felt that I could stay quietly in the background. But by the time Katie had celebrated her second birthday Andrew had started playgroup; Amy and Leigh were both at school and life had settled down to a more ordered routine, with fewer disturbed nights. I found I was being asked to emerge from my shell!

There was no meeting for the younger women – could I start one? The children's holiday club needed helpers; could I give a hand? (I could bring my own children, of course!) Could I speak at the meeting for older women which was held on Wednesdays? Could I visit the local London City Mission hall to talk to the older women's meeting? (My predecessor at the manse had always been happy to . . .) And, worst of all, could I visit one or two sick church folk and pray with them? I didn't like to say "No" to any of these requests; I felt it wouldn't look good for Richard if his wife wasn't seen to be helpful! And I had been a Christian for a long time – surely I *ought* to be able to cope with these things that "went with the job"? Somehow I muddled through; but I knew that I did not know God well enough to be able to communicate his love and power to others. Something was missing.

Asking and receiving

At that point in time I had just begun to pray regularly with Tania, a Christian girl whose husband, Tony, had turned away from the Lord. She came to my house each week and we prayed for him to come back to God. Tania prayed for Tony with tremendous faith, and I felt that she knew the Lord better than I did. One day she spoke about "being baptized in the Holy Spirit" as something she had experienced a long time after her conversion to Christ. I was intrigued; could this be anything to do with my missing "something"? I decided to search the Scriptures for myself.

For the next few weeks I spent every spare minute finding

out about the Holy Spirit. As I read my Bible it became very clear to me that the early Christians experienced the power of the Holy Spirit coming upon them in a definite way which produced immediate consequences in their lives. In Acts 2 the first outpouring of the Spirit changed the disciples from timid, puzzled people into fearless and powerful witnesses for Jesus. The same thing happened in Acts 4:31 when the Spirit filled them again. Later, when Peter and John were in Samaria, they laid hands on the newly converted and baptized Christians, and the Holy Spirit came upon them (Acts 8:14–17).

When Saul was converted on the Damascus road (Acts 9) he was blind for three days. God told Ananias to go to the house where Saul was staying; Ananias obeyed, and when he arrived he said to Saul, "Brother Saul, the Lord – Jesus, who appeared to you on the road as you were coming here – has sent me so that you may see again *and be filled with the Holy Spirit*" (verse 17). When Peter preached in Caesarea (Acts 10) the Holy Spirit fell on the people as they listened and believed. In Acts 19 the Holy Spirit came upon the Ephesian believers following their baptism. My Bible told me that in several of these instances the newly Spirit-filled people "spoke in tongues" or "prophesied". I didn't know what this meant, but by now I knew that I wanted and needed to be baptized in the Holy Spirit as these early believers were. And I wanted whatever went with it, as long as it was biblical! I longed to witness freely for Jesus (something I had always found hard) and I wanted to serve him with power over sin. I knew that my need was great and that I could never support Richard's ministry unless God's power touched my life in a new way.

I became very thirsty! I read the words of Jesus in John 7:37–39 and longed for the water of the Holy Spirit. During

my weeks of searching the Bible, normal life had to carry on.
I cooked meals, ironed clothes, helped with homework, even
spoke at a few meetings – but inside I was becoming more and
more thirsty. I began to ask Jesus to baptize me in his Holy
Spirit. I prayed several times, telling the Lord how much I
needed this baptism of power, why I needed it, that I believed
he wanted to give it to me because it was the Father's promise
(Acts 1:4–5). I kept on and on reminding him of all these
things!

One July morning I was standing in our bedroom after
another "asking" session when I heard the voice of Jesus say
quietly into my heart *"Why don't you stop asking and just
receive?"* Immediately I was silent; I obeyed his voice. When I
stopped striving, he answered my prayer. I opened my heart
to the Spirit of God, and I knew he had come. At that point
in time I didn't feel anything other than a quiet certainty. But
as the day progressed I became aware of the glory of God in
a way I had never known. That afternoon we went out for a
picnic with some friends, and as we walked in the country my
heart felt as if it would burst with praise. Every tree, every
blade of grass spoke to me of the power and love of my Lord.

The next morning, I went downstairs very early to have my
quiet time. As I read my Bible the words came alive to me
with power – this was truly the word of the living God.
Suddenly I could only worship and praise him, pouring out
my love and adoration as I received the revelation of his glory
and love. Eventually, I had to tear myself away; I went upstairs
to wake the children. Richard looked at me curiously. "You've
been downstairs over an hour," he said. It had seemed like five
minutes, and I couldn't wait to get back into the presence of
Jesus. I had told Richard about my decision to search the

Scriptures for information about the Holy Spirit; now I shared with him God's answer to my prayer. (It was to be another year before Richard, together with many others in the church, experienced a similar baptism in the Holy Spirit.)

Walking in the Spirit

Through the following weeks and months my "walk in the Spirit" deepened and strengthened; great joy in the Lord was not something I had ever experienced, but now I found my heart constantly flooded with joy and praise as I read my Bible and prayed. This was a rejoicing in Jesus himself, in all that he now was to me. I understood how Peter had been able to write, "Though you have not seen him, you love him; and even though you do not see him now, you believe in him and are filled with an inexpressible and glorious joy" (1 Peter 1:8). Jesus said of the Holy Spirit, "He will bring glory to me by taking from what is mine and making it known to you" (John 16:14). The Spirit was doing exactly that – revealing to me the wonder and glory of Jesus in a way I had never known before. I could not praise him enough for what he had done in my life; this experience of the Spirit had had a profound effect upon my life; my attitudes to many things had changed radically, especially in the area of relationships. The baptism in the Spirit softens and prepares the soil for the fruit of the Spirit to grow more easily!

One evening a few weeks later, Tania's husband Tony came to see Richard, and during that evening he gave his life back to the Lord. Richard called me into the sitting-room, where they had been praying, and we all rejoiced. Before Tony left, we prayed together. Tania had told me that Tony, until he went away from God, had been a committed and Spirit-filled

Christian. Now, as we prayed, Tony began to speak in another language. It was not a language I recognized, and I realized that this must be praying "in tongues". I had never heard anything like it before, but my heart lifted as I listened to Tony pouring out his praise to God for welcoming him back.

The next day, I was thinking about this matter of "tongues" and tentatively said to the Lord, "I would love to praise you like that." Within minutes some words formed in my mind – I could see them clearly and knew I should speak them out. I did so, and more words formed on the screen of my mind as if I were reading an autocue! The words I saw were in a language which was nothing like Tony's beautiful prayer the previous evening, and I wondered if I could be making it up; yet it seemed to have come as the Lord's answer to what I had said to him. I carried on using the words that came to me, and over the next few weeks the language expanded and I found myself using it to praise and pray. One day I was reading Psalm 139, and verse 4 came to me very strongly, "Before a word is on my tongue you know it completely, O Lord." After that I ceased worrying – I knew God had given me this gift and wanted me to use it.

The baptism is a beginning

In the early church the baptism in the Spirit was part of Christian initiation, in the same way as water baptism. This is obvious as we read the New Testament. But because this has not been the case in most denominations of the present-day church, some of us had to wait a long time before we experienced it! Thankfully, that is not the case now; many churches are open to the baptism and gifts of the Spirit. These gifts, mentioned in Romans 12 and I Corinthians 14, are for the building up of the church. The baptism in the Holy Spirit is the doorway into the supernatural dimension of our Christian faith. But we don't stay in the doorway! As we walk in the Spirit, using his gifts and allowing his fruit to be produced in our lives (Galatians 5:22), we will be available for God to use us in our families, among our friends and in our churches.

One of the wonderful things God did for me through the baptism in the Spirit was to bring reality and honesty into my life. He showed me the greatness of his love by pouring out his Spirit upon me, and thus assuring me that I was accepted and loved in spite of my unworthiness and many failings. His power in my life meant that I could begin to change. I no longer felt that I had to behave in a certain way because I was the pastor's wife. I could be me! This brought freedom into my life, and I was much more relaxed. I could even say "No" when asked to speak at meetings! I didn't have to rush round tidying up if someone was about to call. Everyone knew that I had four lively children; they wouldn't expect me to be Superwoman. Because the Lord loved and accepted me I could trust people to do the same. The Holy Spirit in my life was the Attitude-changer *par excellence*!

As you have been reading this, perhaps God has spoken to you. Have you experienced the baptism in the Holy Spirit? If you haven't, or if you have never realized that this is for you, spend some time looking at the scriptures mentioned in this section. Ask God to show you his truth – and ask him to make you thirsty! Perhaps you feel (or have even been taught) that "baptism in the Holy Spirit" is not biblical teaching but a false doctrine taught by those whose desire is to whip up emotional and noisy meetings. The Bible tells us that Jesus is the one who baptizes with the Holy Spirit (John 1:33). Go to him and ask him to confirm this as truth or falsehood in your heart. He will!

Prayer – communication with God

Receiving the baptism in the Holy Spirit will increase your desire to spend time with Jesus, to worship and praise him, and to be intimate with God our Father, his Son and his Spirit in a new way.

Some years ago my daughter Leigh and I stayed up all night to talk. Leigh wanted to discuss whether or not she should begin a relationship with Martin, a friend who was interested in being more than a friend to her. She was interested in him, too, but not sure about taking matters any further. She needed to talk, and I, as her mum, wanted to listen. We didn't start to talk until eleven o'clock in the evening – so we simply carried on through the night. The result of our long conversation was the beginning of a relationship which resulted in a wedding the following year! Prayer is like that. God wants to hear about our cares and concerns because he is our loving Father. He wants to help us resolve issues and sort out situations in our lives. He is willing and glad to listen to us at any hour of the day or night. But, unlike we human parents who cannot always find answers for our children, our loving Father is Almighty God. He has power to answer prayer, change situations and lift burdens. And because he is our sovereign God, he has power to give us peace in situations where his purposes for us involve a learning curve, where he will not necessarily change a situation but will change us instead.

There are many books about prayer, and this is not a "how-to" manual, so I am only going to mention two aspects of prayer, both of which are affected by our attitudes. They are *intimacy* and *intercession*.

Intimacy with God

Above all else, our God longs for intimacy with us, his children. Prayer is the means by which this intimacy happens, and prayer is also the result of intimacy. Our desire to pray is linked to the level of our intimacy with him. (That's not to say we only pray when we feel "intimate" with him; there are times when we pray because we discipline ourselves to do so.)

I often tell Richard how much I love him, and he often tells me the same. If the communication of human love brings such joy, how much more can we enjoy the Lord's communication of his love to us – and how much must he enjoy the communication of our love to him? We can rest in his presence and enjoy his love, knowing that he understands us totally and loves us unconditionally. Responding to his love with adoration and thanksgiving, worship and trust will increase our intimacy with him. We can praise him in tongues as well as our own language, we can sing to him – and we can listen to him. He wants to communicate with us, and if we wait in his presence we will hear his voice; not usually audibly, but deep within us we will know he has spoken. Sometimes a verse of scripture will come strongly to us, sometimes a vision or picture, sometimes just an impression of his love or a sense of security in belonging to him. At times he may give us his answer to a problem we have brought to him.

We can continue intimacy with him through the day as we recognize his presence with us. While we are working outside the home, or looking after small children in the home, there is not much opportunity for being "in prayer". But we can enjoy fellowship with Jesus as we get on with our routine tasks. I remember an occasion some years ago when I was busy cooking. It was during the school holidays, and I had settled the children in the next room to "make things" from a pile of old boxes and cartons (*à la Blue Peter*) while I rushed around in the kitchen. I had planned to pray for some specific people while I was cooking, thus killing several birds with one stone! But each time I began to pray as I measured out ingredients, one or other of the children would come in and interrupt me with a request for advice or admiration depending on how their "construction" was coming on. Frustration caused my replies to become shorter and sharper each time a little visitor appeared, and in the end I gave up the struggle and asked the Lord to forgive my impatience and just to let me enjoy him as I worked. He answered my prayer and I had a wonderful time in his presence as I finished the cooking.

Desire for God will lead to intimacy, and intimacy will produce increased desire to know him better. But perhaps the thought of intimacy with God is not something which "grabs" you? Is your reaction a negative one? You will not find it easy to be intimate with a God who seems distant or unapproachable and in whose presence you feel unworthy or awkward in spite of your experience of his salvation and forgiveness. Read again through the sections, "The reality of God's grace" and "The power of the Holy Spirit". Perhaps you have not yet entered into your inheritance as a child of God. Let his word speak to your heart, and recognize how much he loves you and desires intimacy with you. Let the Holy Spirit change your attitude!

Intimacy affects intercession

Intimacy with God increases our knowledge and awareness of his will, and this awareness helps our intercession for ourselves and for others. 1 John 5:14–15 says, "This is the confidence we have in approaching God: that if we ask anything *according to his will*, he hears us. And if we know that he hears us – whatever we ask – we know that we have what we asked of him."

Intimacy with God also increases our faith in his love and power, so that when we come to intercede for people and situations, we are able to call on him with an attitude of trust in his ordering of the outcome. When difficult and desperate events occur in our lives or the lives of our loved ones we can come to him knowing that his love only wants what is best for his children. Faith-filled intercession is dependent upon intimacy; they are inextricably linked.

Intercession – the practicalities

Unless we are in an unusual situation, ordinary life for most women cannot involve hours and hours of prayer. And if we only have a limited time it is better to use it for intimacy rather than intercession, though we will find at times that one will lead to the other. There are practical ways of building intercession into our lives. You can pray in the car, and if you make a journey on a regular basis you can use different parts of your journey to intercede for different matters (but do watch the road as well!). Most of my intercessory prayer happens when I go for an early morning walk several times a week. When you are ironing clothes you can pray for the wearer of each item of clothing. My three daughters all took over their personal ironing when they reached their teens, so I had to make sure they received my "praying time" to make up for it!

We keep photographs in every room of our house and I use them as prayer reminders. My friend Maggie is a teacher in West Africa; her photo on my kitchen notice-board reminds me to pray for her. My friend Angela lives in East Anglia where she works among overseas students at the university, befriending them and running Bible studies and social activities for them. Angela's photograph is on my notice-board too, and that of my friend Rosemary who is involved in healthcare and literacy work in India. They need my prayers and I'm reminded to pray for them when I go into the kitchen in the morning to put the kettle on. In our previous church we had one wall of the downstairs toilet completely covered with photos of church members, and these were a constant reminder to pray for our brothers and sisters. One of our young people didn't like the photo of her we had put up; she insisted on bringing round another one which showed her "best side". Our wall of photographs frequently kept people in there for long sessions!

How should we intercede?

We will know the prayer needs of our close family members, from teething and playgroup problems through to school, college and work. Our friends will usually let us know if there are specific matters for prayer, and if we have family or friends on the mission field or in other Christian work there will be newsletters or email to keep us informed. But there is one passage of scripture which I think of as an "intercession aid". It is Paul's prayer for the Colossians in chapter 1:9–14. Have a look at it! We can pray this passage every time we intercede for ourselves, for our families and friends, for our brothers and sisters in Christ and any others for whom we pray – even our enemies, those who are against us (Matthew 5:44). Paul is telling the Colossian church that his unceasing prayer for them is that they may have spiritual wisdom and understanding which leads to a knowledge of God's will, and that they may live a life pleasing to Jesus, bearing fruit and growing in the knowledge of God, and that they may be strengthened by the power of God to have endurance, patience and a heart of thanksgiving for the wonderful salvation into which he has brought them. How's that for an "attitude-changer"?

No matter what situation we are interceding for in a person's life, this prayer is one that God delights to answer. It's a risky prayer; if we pray for patience and endurance to increase in us or in someone we love, God may allow trials and difficulties to bring about the answer to that prayer. We can't learn endurance without having to endure, and we can't learn patience without being in situations where we would naturally be *im*patient!

There will be times when we want to intercede for our town, our nation or our world. (A local or national newspaper is useful here – it stays around longer than a television news report.) Sometimes we will be praying against the activity of the enemy in a local or national situation. I remember when our church prayed against the planned opening of a "sex shop" in a local high street (it foundered well before opening day), and I also remember praying for a number of local Christians who took a stand outside a nearby cinema showing a particularly blasphemous occult horror film. They gave out leaflets warning people about the dangers of occult activity. Intercession of this kind is spiritual warfare, and we will often find ourselves praying in tongues, as we may in any situation where we are not sure of the details or of how to pray. Intercession for our children in their school, college or work environments, where they face many challenges and need the protection of God, will often cause us to use this gift of the Holy Spirit; it gives us the ability to pray with power into unknown situations (especially when we are praying for a teenager who doesn't talk much!).

God loves us to come to him as dependent children with our needs and concerns. "Let us then approach the throne of grace with confidence, so that we may receive mercy and find grace to help us in our time of need" (Hebrews 4:16).

The church, God's family

"Family" is vitally important. We are the result of our roots. Many adopted children, when they become adults, will spend time and money searching for their biological parents. The failure of our family to own, support and strengthen us, to affirm and validate us, can cause many problems in our life and relationships.

When our human family lets us down, we are deeply aware inside us that the situation is not right. Hurts from family members cause far more pain than hurts from outsiders, because we have an innate awareness that "family" should mean love and support. My husband, Richard, lost contact with his father, brother and sister when his parents' marriage failed. At that time the family lived in Manchester and his mother made a sudden decision to leave his father and go to London, taking nine-year-old Richard with her. She left a note for her two other children, twelve-year-old twins, to find when they returned from school that day, telling them that she was leaving to join her new boyfriend.

From that day onwards, neither Richard's father nor his brother and sister made any attempt to contact him or his mother. The difficulties of coping with his new life and school in London, the loss of his family and grandparents, the problems of relating to his new "dad" proved almost too much over the next few years, and in his early teens he was tempted several times to end his life. Later he joined the Army and, after training, was sent to the Far East as a photographic cartographer with a map-making unit. While in Singapore he heard the gospel and gave his life to Jesus. Becoming part of God's family meant that he now had a loving heavenly Father, as well as many new brothers and sisters in Christ. God also brought him into contact with godly older men who "fathered" him in his new Christian life. A few years later he acquired a wife and, over the next seven years, four children. But still the longing to know his real father remained.

One day, when Richard was in his 40s, he received a telephone call telling him that his father had died. He wept and wept. He had known so little of his earthly father, and now he would never know him. A few years later Richard's mother died. He sent a message to someone who had contact with his brother and sister, so that they could be informed of their mother's death. Within hours his brother telephoned him. "We want to see you now and get to know you," said Roderick. "We couldn't do it while Mother was alive, because we never wanted to see her again after the pain she caused us. But we know it wasn't your fault. Can we get together?"

Richard was overjoyed at the reunion with his brother and sister, both now married with families of their own. All three

of them had a lifetime of news to hear, and our children discovered that they had two sets of cousins they hadn't known
existed! Best of all, Richard was able to have photographs of
his father and to learn what he was really like. But the one
question which he needed to ask was, "Why didn't Dad try to
get in touch with me?" The only answer seemed to be that he
was determined not to have any further contact with his wife,
and to make contact with Richard he would have had to go
through her. He was prepared to sacrifice Richard in order to
keep to his principle of non-forgiveness.

Being part of God's family has enabled Richard to receive
healing from the pain of his own birth-family's failure to sustain and support him. The love of his heavenly Father is a reality in his life and has enabled him to be a good and loving
father to his own children. "Family" is part of the wonderful
resources God has for us. Your brothers and sisters in Christ
are the ones who will be committed to you, who will be your
friends, who will support you when you need help, who will
pray for your children, and who will pray for and befriend
your husband if he is not yet a believer. You may have a helpful and supportive natural family, but the family of God will
still be there for you!

Your attitude to the family of God

The attitude you have to your local church "family" is important. Being part of a church which worships together and
cares for one another is vital for our growth as Christians. In
1 Corinthians 12 the apostle Paul makes a comparison of the
church with a human body. He shows clearly how each part is
necessary for the proper working of the body: "Now the body
is not made up of one part, but of many. If the foot should say

'Because I am not a hand, I do not belong to the body', it would not for that reason cease to be part of the body. And if the ear should say 'Because I am not an eye, I do not belong to the body', it would not for that reason cease to be part of the body. If the whole body were an eye, where would the sense of hearing be? If the whole body were an ear, where would the sense of smell be? But in fact God has arranged the parts in the body, every one of them, just as he wanted them to be. If they were all one part, where would the body be? As it is, there are many parts, but one body. The eye cannot say to the hand, 'I don't need you!' And the head cannot say to the feet, 'I don't need you!'" (1 Corinthians 12:14–21). In the same passage Paul describes our commitment to one another: "If one part suffers, every part suffers with it; if one part is honoured, every part rejoices with it. Now you are the body of Christ, and each one of you is a part of it" (1 Corinthians 12:26–27).

How is your own commitment to the family of God? In several of his other epistles Paul shows the kind of attitudes and behaviour we should have towards one another. Look up these verses and instead of reading them as demands being made upon *you*, see yourself as the recipient – of all this devotion, honour, love, acceptance, patience, kindness, encouragement, etc. . . . God wants you to have all this and give it back to others!

"Be devoted to one another in brotherly love" (Romans 12:10)

"Honour one another above yourselves" (Romans 12:10)

"Love one another" (Romans 13:8)

"Accept one another" (Romans 15:7)

"Serve one another" (Galatians 5:13)

"Be patient, bearing with one another in love" (Ephesians 4:2)

"Be kind and compassionate to one another" (Ephesians 4:32)

"Submit to one another" (Ephesians 5:21)

"Encourage one another and build each other up" (1 Thessalonians 5:11)

We can see that these attitudes toward one another will not allow us to be independent; functioning as part of God's family is important for us. We all enjoy watching the television antics of Mr Bean, who has no family and relates only to his brown teddy bear, on whom he lavishes a peculiar form of love and care. Clearly, Mr Bean has no idea how to relate to real people! When we become part of God's family, he wants us to share our lives; independence is not an option. Somebody once said that Christians are to be like mashed potatoes, not snooker balls; we are to be involved with one another in unity and love. "I keep myself to myself" is a character trait which has no place in the life of a Christian. Jesus said that our unity and love as the family of God would be the visible proof that God had sent him (John 17:23). Satan will do his utmost to destroy family life, both in the natural and in the spiritual sense. We have all met families where one member is "not speaking" to another because of a disagreement between them.

When we become part of the Christian family we find ourselves with brothers and sisters we would not necessarily have chosen as part of our life. We may find it hard to get on with some of them; they will not always do things the way we do, or treat us as we feel we should be treated. But God brings us into his family in order to change us – and he will change other people through us, just as he changes us through other people. His aim is to make all of us like Jesus. The more we become like him, the better we will relate to one another. Do you have an attitude which prevents you being fully integrated with God's family where you are? Is there someone you don't relate to because her "social standing" is not the same as yours? Someone who brings up her children in a different way from you? A leader who doesn't lead as you think he should?

When Richard was reunited with his brother Roderick, he found that there were many similarities between them, though they had lived apart from one another for 39 years. They are both very good at table tennis and they both like weak tea. They both enjoy painting pictures, as does their sister Rosemary. There is a physical family likeness, too; it is obvious that they have the same father and mother. God wants his children's parentage to be obvious, too, as they become visibly more and more like Jesus.

Where do you go from here?

As you read the rest of this book, especially as you look at the "season" in which you are now living, you will have some choices to make. If you have read these foundational chapters with an open heart, you will already know if there are attitudes in your life which need to change. Your commitment to change will be challenged – you have an enemy who will try to keep you as you are! If you are holding on to past hurts and resentments Satan will persuade you that these are important to you, at the same time as the voice of Jesus will be calling you to let them go.

Change requires you to be single-minded and focused in your choices. How will you use your time? What will you read and watch? Our thinking is affected by what goes into our minds. What are your priorities and values? Have certain goals or values infiltrated your life to handicap your witness and your growth in God? The prophet Isaiah, writing about the sad state of God's people, says their "choice wine is diluted" (Isaiah 1:22). That's a powerful metaphor – a good wine diluted with water is not worth drinking! Your Christian life can become "diluted" if other priorities have lessened your commitment to Jesus. But God wants to change your attitudes, renew your mind and make you like his Son. Will you let him?

To consider: If you recognized any inappropriate attitudes in your life after reading chapter 1, can you see in chapter 2 any particular truth to apply to your life?

CHAPTER THREE

SEASONS OF SINGLENESS

Some years ago I was praying with a Christian friend who found her singleness very difficult to handle. She felt held back in life by her lack of a partner and her longing to be married. As we prayed God gave me a picture of a tilted salt-cellar with a stream of salt pouring out, and words for my friend that her singleness did not prevent her being "salt and light" in her community. As we finished praying she looked up and asked anxiously, "Did you see a pepper-pot next to the salt-cellar?"

Another friend, Ruth, told me about the time she shared a tent at a summer Bible Week with three girls who were all showing off engagement rings and discussing their marriage plans. "I felt so alone," she said. "I wanted to be engaged, too – but I wasn't. I wasn't even 'going out' with a bloke! It was hard."

For many singles, "bridesmaiding" has become more and more difficult as they see their friends marrying while they remain single. Some have even refused wedding invitations because they cannot bear to listen to the words of the marriage service one more time.

Many of us grow up with a strong desire for marriage, and if we are Christians we want a godly husband who will lead us in following Jesus. If you are past your 20s and had expected to be married by now, you may have questions in your mind: Will marriage ever happen for me? My strong desire for marriage doesn't go away – why hasn't God brought me a Christian husband? Is there something wrong with me? Have I offended God in some way? I must be a failure; nobody wants me.

The fact is that in the United Kingdom 24% of the adults in evangelical churches are single women and 11% of them are single men. This huge differential indicates that there will be a number of women who will not find a partner.

In this chapter we will look at aspects of singleness: its joys, pressures and dilemmas, and see how we can have positive attitudes as single people walking with God.

Pressure points

Loneliness

"The loneliness is the worst part of being single," says my friend Rosie, who is in her early 30s. Rosie's early life was marred by broken family relationships and years in a children's care home after her mother abandoned her. In her mid-teens life became more stable when she went to live with her father and her new stepmother, with whom she had a good relationship, and becoming a Christian brought her into a relationship with God. After university and college she came to live near us in south London.

Rosie talked to me honestly about her feelings: "I assumed

I would get married by my mid-20s. Before I became a Christian, I was in a relationship for several years. Since knowing the Lord I haven't had a boyfriend. I want to marry a Christian man and have a family of my own. I enjoy my job and I love my flat but I know that if I were married I would give up being career-minded. Almost all the friends I used to socialize with are now married or engaged. Each time it happens, I find it hard. Obviously I'm happy for them (and I really am!), but sometimes I find myself saying to God, '*Why* am I still single when I want so much to be married?' At times I wonder if I'm being punished for something – but I know God isn't like that. Yes, I do still hope to marry. I'm getting on with my life, but I do want a Christian husband and I'm praying that God will bring someone into my life. I'm not naïve enough to think that marriage will be perfect but I really do want a partner to share life with."

Rosie feels that being single in your 20s is different from being single in your 30s. "There's a different agenda. In your 20s everything is more casual; you can take a long time getting to know someone. When you get to your 30s, and people around you are settling down, you can almost hear your biological clock ticking! When you meet someone, you know very quickly if you want it to continue."

Rosie's comment on marriage is realistic. How do *you* view marriage? Do you see it as the panacea for all ills, the antidote to loneliness, or something that will give you far more status than singleness? Do you feel that marriage will prove that you are worth loving? All these are false assumptions and are often present as a result of rejection or abuse in earlier years. If this is your situation, dealing properly with your past, perhaps with the help of a Christian counsellor, will prepare you for a more realistic view of marriage. If you see marriage as something that will bring you acceptance, stability and direction for your life, recognize that these are all needs for your single life, too. In chapter 1, I referred to women who entered marriage with unreal expectations, assuming that a Christian husband would meet their needs, solve their problems and give them a new identity and self-image as well as a wonderful life for ever after. The reality is that only one person can do that, and his name is Jesus. Learning to delight yourself in him, whether you marry or not, will enable your heart's needs to be met.

Will I ever hold my own child?

For some single women, the desire for a baby of their own is a very powerful drive towards marriage. One of my close friends told me that if she had not married by the time she was 30 she would have been seriously tempted to go out and get herself pregnant, so strong was her desire for a child. Another friend, Elizabeth, who is now in her late 30s and still unmarried, spoke to me of her own longing for a child. "I was talking with a married friend last year," she said. "She's had several miscarriages and was desperate for a baby. She knows how much I want to get married and she said to me that she thought my desire for marriage was similar to her deep desire for a baby. We both wanted what we couldn't have. Three weeks ago she had a lovely baby boy – so her longing is satisfied." Elizabeth wiped the tears from her eyes. "Her baby is a miracle and I am really happy for her. But I so much want children – and a husband! I know that the older I get the less chance I have."

For many older single women the menopause is a painful milestone. It signals the death of hope, when a woman is bereaved of babies longed for but never conceived or born. Every bereavement involves grief, and menopausal grief is very real; it may bring a renewed questioning of God's sovereignty and his purposes. Coming to a place of trust in him is important, as Angela commented (see the later section, "Older singles").

Unfulfilled expectations

Like Rosie and Angela, Elizabeth expected to marry and have a family. "I expected to be married by my mid-20s. Then I expected it by my 30s. Now I'm *in* my 30s and I still expect it to happen but I'm not putting a time on it!"

Elizabeth had found men difficult to understand and relate to, as her father had left home when she was seven. She had had boyfriends during her teen years, including a couple who were "serious". She became a Christian in her late teens and was always part of a group of friends who did things together. Elizabeth, who has a beautiful Scots accent, went to university in Glasgow and then moved to Edinburgh for two years before coming down south to work. After several moves she found herself living in a flat near her present church and, at the invitation of a friend, began to attend services and was soon feeling at home and making friends in the church. She was asked out by a male friend at church but the relationship did not work and only lasted a short time before he left the church. Another relationship followed but again did not last. "It was too intense; he became obsessed with me. He said God had told him he would marry me!" (This kind of "personal prophecy" should be viewed with extreme caution and checked out with your pastor or church leader – especially if it comes from someone who wants a relationship with you.)

A year or two later Elizabeth became involved with Bill, a young man to whom she was very attracted. He is a member of a church on the south coast, and they met through mutual Christian friends. Elizabeth fell deeply in love, knowing that Bill was someone she wanted to marry. They became good friends, and he would share his problems and difficulties with her. But the relationship never led to marriage, though it continued, on and off, for many years. "It was as if Bill could not commit himself to marriage," said Elizabeth. "He had a lot of problems which he needed to sort out, but that never happened, and the problems seemed to prevent him coming to any kind of commitment. Either that or he didn't love me as much as I loved him! I was confused. I know I should have broken it off with him, but somehow I couldn't; I was completely weak and helpless because of my love for him, even though I could see that our relationship was going nowhere. I also knew that God was telling me to end it and move on – he had given me scriptures that clearly confirmed it.

"Eventually I tried to stop seeing Bill, but after a few months we resumed contact and it all started again. I went and talked to my pastor about the situation; he realized how weak I was against the attraction of this man. I said I wanted to finish the relationship, so he phoned Bill's pastor, who spoke to Bill, and we agreed to stop seeing each other. For a long time we had no contact at all. Then, last year, we began to see each other again. I had been leading a cell-group at church but I gave that up because of him. My relationship with God suffered – all that mattered to me was seeing Bill. I didn't want to carry on in this inconclusive way but I seemed trapped in this relationship with him.

"Then one day Naomi, a friend who had deputized for me

in leading my cell-group, asked if she could help in any way, as she could see that I was unhappy. I decided to trust her, and shared my situation with her. She asked if I had ever heard the term "soul-ties" – spiritual links which bind one person to another in an unhelpful way, as a result of a strong but unhealthy emotional attachment or some other factor. I had not, but as she talked with me I recognized that this was probably true of my relationship with Bill. Later, Naomi prayed with me to break this tie. Nothing dramatic happened but the tie was definitely broken and there has been a significant difference. I've now stayed away from him for a long time and I've even been out with someone else once or twice – though it didn't come to anything; I didn't really want it to. I wonder if I will ever get over Bill completely and be able to have another relationship. I find it difficult to understand why God allowed this to happen in my life. But thankfully I am now walking closely with God. He has helped me to be content in my present situation and I'm trusting him for a future partner. I have a lovely network of friends who are really important to me and I want to maintain those friendships. I do find it increasingly hard when friends get married and enter the "world of couples". It feels sometimes as if I'm sitting in a waiting-room!"

Remaining in an inconclusive and static relationship because it seems better than no relationship at all can be counter-productive, taking up time and emotional energy and leaving no freedom for new relationships to develop.

For some single women who expect to marry there can be a sense of life being "on hold" or "in a waiting-room", as Elizabeth put it, and the temptation is to look forward to the future rather than living positively in the present. If you are in this situation you may find yourself "holding back" from opportunities in case you miss a chance with somebody you find attractive. But Jesus tells us to live for today and to recognize that our Father *will* supply our needs – not only for material necessities, but also for those things which are "more important" than food and clothing (Matthew 6:25–26). Our Lord wants us to live in the present with contentment, not "marking time" while we wait for our knight in shining armour (or Armani suit and matching Porsche!) to arrive. You can choose, quite deliberately, to live in the NOW – enjoying your life, your relationship with God, your friends, your church, your interests. You can be celibate – for today. You can focus on serving Jesus – for today.

If God's present plan for you is a single life, see the opportunities and advantages of it. This is a time when you can grow spiritually as you spend time learning the ways of God by reading his word and having fellowship with him. You can grow creatively in your chosen interest, whether it is learning another language, collecting old china or taking a car maintenance course (perhaps that worrying noise in your car engine will become less mysterious!). It is a time when you are free to travel or move for the sake of the kingdom of God, and to give more money to God's work. It's a time to get to know and value yourself, to recognize and build up your strengths and work on your weaknesses.

Sexuality

What do you do about expressing your sexuality? As a single Christian woman you can't indulge in casual sex or even sex with a serious boyfriend. The Bible tells us that sex is for marriage, so if you aren't married do you have to repress the sexual side of your nature? Can you be a whole woman without a man? The answer to that is a resounding "Yes!" Don't confuse sexuality with the act of sexual intercourse. The fact that, as an unmarried Christian, you don't engage in sex does not mean that you give up on being a woman. You are a whole person, a whole woman – not half a person, a salt-cellar waiting for a pepper-pot before she can function properly! God did not create you incomplete.

Satan will tell you that you cannot get by without sex, if not with a real man then by proxy as you watch films, visit internet sites or read books which arouse you sexually, leading to masturbation or to actual fornication. The more you indulge in sexual viewing and reading, the more easily you will be tempted, and there will always be men willing to help you yield (sadly, sometimes Christian men – a man's character is not always in line with his Christian commitment). Giving in to sexual temptation will prevent you growing as a Christian. If this is a problem for you, bring it "into the light". Share your difficulties with a trusted Christian woman friend who will pray with you and hold you accountable. You cannot live a double life – you either delight yourself in Christ or delight yourself in illicit sex. It's a straight choice.

The practicalities of life

You want to book a holiday in Italy – but you don't have anyone to go with and you don't feel you can ask around, in case everybody has already booked up. You have a long form to fill in from the tax office, and you can't make any sense of it. The toilet floods and you don't know how to fix it. There's that mysterious noise coming from the car engine – you hope it's nothing serious, but you're not sure. Oh, for a husband!

As my friend Alice says, it's often the practical things that bring singleness home to you. There are so many areas where the lack of a partner hurts deeply. After all, just having someone to sort out the car would save your financial situation. And setting up home for the first time is expensive when you don't have all those wedding presents!

These are the times to remember that you are part of the body of Christ. You may not have a husband, but you do have brothers and sisters! There are men and women in your church who understand toilets and cars. Singles sometimes complain that churches are family orientated and that they feel left out. But the church *is* family, and if we have needs to be met and disasters to be coped with, the family is where we should look for help. If you can summon up the courage to ask for help with a problem, a friendship will grow, and the time will come when you are able to give help in return. (An observation here: some husbands will happily go and help single friends when their wives are begging them to do urgent jobs in their own homes. This kind of help will not improve your friendship with the wife or their relationship as a couple. Be wise about where you ask for help!)

You may need to guard yourself against resentment that your married friends assume you are always free to babysit and your church leaders assume that you are always free to be involved in church commitments, yet you still have a demanding job, a home to run, washing, ironing, cleaning, gardening, shopping and cooking – and no partner to share the chores!

If you are a divorced single woman with children (like Rosemary in a later section, "Becoming single again") you will be faced with the task of parenting on your own, and we will explore that more fully in the next chapter.

Family and peer pressures

Parents want the best for their children, and most parents want the best possible partner for their daughter. Many mothers want to think "weddings" followed by "grandchildren"! This can be a great pressure on single daughters, and family weddings can become painful episodes with comments about catching the bride's bouquet and discussions about who will be next. As time goes by, there may be insinuations that something is wrong or that you are too choosy – especially if your parents are not Christians.

My own parents, who were very opposed to church and Christians, were extremely taken aback when I was converted to Christ in my early teens. For several years they insisted that it was "a phase I was going through" and that I would "grow out of it eventually". They were painful years. I met Richard when I was 20, and within weeks we knew that we would marry. My parents, especially my mother, were horrified when they realized that he, too, was a committed Christian. Now there was no chance that I would "grow out of it". They were torn between pleasure that I was actually getting married (they had thought that no one would want to marry a "religious nut"!) and the recognition that if I was marrying Richard, whom they liked, I was certainly going to remain a Christian. "Growing out of it" was no longer up for discussion! Family pressure can be difficult.

Has pressure affected your relationship with your engaged and married friends? Are you relaxed and free with them or do you find that jealousies creep in, as well as resentment that they are not so available to spend time with you now that they are building marriages, making homes and having babies?

Perhaps they tried to "matchmake" for you at first but none of the men they introduced to you wanted a relationship, except the one you didn't like! Now you only seem to socialize with groups of single friends at church and the people you know at work. You babysit for married friends and often they invite you for a meal first, so the friendship is still there. But somehow, as time goes by, it becomes more difficult.

If you recognize within yourself a longing for a marriage partner, is this a pressure that affects your relationships with men? Are you over-eager and anxious to please, rather than relaxed and at peace with your male friends? Can you enjoy the friendship and companionship of men friends without being either "come hither" or aggressive in your interaction with them?

Having looked at some of the pressures, let's look at the kind of positive action you can take to counteract them.

Positive action for the down times

Preparing a strategy

Self-pity is an ever-present enemy when you are feeling "down". Recognize times when you are particularly vulnerable (just after a friend's wedding, just before a period . . .) and prepare a strategy. If you are aware of feeling especially vulnerable at *any* time, steer clear of romantic films and fiction.

Make a list of scriptures that emphasize your security in God and the fact that you are special to him (see chapter 2). Reaffirm your trust in his sovereignty over your life. In his will *at this present time* you are single. Jesus says to you, as he said to John the Baptist in prison when John was doubting his authenticity (Matthew 11:6), "Blessed is the man [*or woman*] who does not fall away on account of me." Ask his forgiveness for any resentment against him about your situation. Jesus was himself single, and he totally understands how you feel. (He never even had a home – Luke 9:58.) Remember that "we do not have a high priest who is unable to sympathize with our weaknesses, but we have one who has been tempted in every way, just as we are" (Hebrews 4:15). You can have a relationship with him which is completely open about the sins, fears and pressures connected with your singleness, and by seeing how he related to people and situations and how he depended on his Father for guidance and strength, you can learn how to live in peace.

Value yourself

"I don't feel special"; "Nobody's chosen me" – I have often heard single folk say this and it is obviously a real source of pain. But remember that you *are* special – to God, to your family, your friends and your church. Recognize your own value. First, keep yourself in the love of God (Jude 21) and value your intimacy with him (see chapter 2 again!). Second, remember that you have an enemy who will seek to play on your emotions to isolate you from God and from fellowship with other Christians; take positive action to counteract Satan's tactics. Go and seek out a good friend for a hug and a chat; be open about how you feel.

Value yourself in positive ways. Look after yourself; treat yourself on a regular basis to something you enjoy – a bunch of flowers, a new book, a beauty treatment. Go to an aerobics or dance class (or if you can't manage that, put on some lively music and boogie in your sitting-room for 20 minutes!). Make a list of recipes that you enjoy, and cook yourself a special meal once a week. Have a joint party with someone whose birthday is near yours. Single folk don't have wedding anniversaries, but you can celebrate other special days – invite one or more friends over to join you, and cook a meal or have a take-away. Even if it is the end of the month, soup and rolls look good with candles. And a late-evening picnic in the park is enjoyable in summer. My friend Liz often invites friends for Saturday breakfast!

Keep a list of "things to do when feeling down". This can include practical jobs to do in the house, places to visit (go on your own or phone and invite a friend) and people who need help or encouragement; sometimes, helping someone else will help to eliminate "the blues".

When friends marry

Prepare an "emotional strategy" for the time when you are missing your best friend who has just got married. Yes, your relationship with her will change, and you may find that difficult. For a time you may feel she has withdrawn from you, but the reality is that she will need to devote her emotional energy to establishing the new husband/wife relationship. Recognize this, and give her time – she *will* come back to your friendship, and you will enjoy her company again. But it is important that you acknowledge her new situation – she is still your friend, but her primary relationship now is that of wife to her husband. When she chooses to spend time with him rather than with you, don't react with jealousy and resentment. She will have to organize her time much more than before, and it may take a while to establish a routine which allows for all the new demands of husband, home, work, church and friendships. You may need to plan times together in advance rather than meeting as a result of a spontaneous phone call.

You may want to rethink how deeply you will share with her, if her husband is her chief "confidant". And likewise, she may not feel it is appropriate to share with you on the same level as she did before. Don't be thrown by these factors and don't let the devil isolate you and cause you to doubt the wisdom of forming close and loving friendships if they are going to cease when one of you marries. Your friendship won't cease but will change and develop, as all relationships do. If you have had a very exclusive friendship this can be painful, but it can also be a springboard for recognizing your need to develop other satisfying friendships and interests.

Being pro-active

If God has put a strong desire for marriage within you, be prepared to act positively in terms of meeting people. It seems illogical to say at the age of 70, "Yes, I would have liked to marry but the right man just never came along", if you have never gone looking! In recent years I have known several Christian women who have married men who are not Christians. None of the Christian men in their churches had shown any interest in them, and they had met men outside the church who had made it clear that they were not only interested but attracted. Relationships had developed, leading to marriage plans. The men were happy for their future wives to continue going to church, though they themselves were not at all interested in attending, except for the wedding service.

Is this the only choice – that a Christian woman with a strong desire for marriage must, if no suitable Christian man is available in her church or friendship circle, either remain single or marry an unbeliever? And is a Christian woman whose career requires frequent relocation and unsociable working hours, and who finds it difficult to settle and get to know people because of frequent church changes, faced with the same dilemma? The good news is that there are other options. It's possible to be introduced to a partner through a Christian introduction or dating agency.

Dating agencies

If we want a particular job situation, we put together a *curriculum vitae* and fill in application forms. If we want a new car we look in the appropriate paper or magazine. If we want to sell a house we don't sit at home waiting for a buyer: we put the house in the hands of an efficient estate agent. I am convinced that a good Christian dating agency can be of immense value to Christian singles of both sexes.

A friend who leads a church near us was telling us recently of two people in his congregation who have used a dating agency. One man who did so was a young businessman whose high-flying job in the city left him no time to socialize in ways that would enable him to meet a Christian girl. He wanted a Christian marriage and therefore approached a Christian agency (which was duly checked out by our friend, his pastor!). The agency is one which takes careful profiles of its clients and prays about every introduction made, as well as giving advice on establishing a successful relationship. The first girl to whom he was introduced proved exactly right for him, and they are now happily married. The second church member who used the agency was a shy girl who found it difficult to make individual relationships, though she was happy in a group. Wanting to meet a Christian partner, she registered with the same dating agency (again with the full agreement of her pastor!) and was matched with a similarly shy young man whom she eventually married and with whom she is very happy.

In a recent issue of the magazine *Woman Alive* journalist Catherine Francis interviewed Mychelle, who had met her husband Mike through The Network, an agency which arranges various events and holidays for single, widowed and divorced Christians, plus personal introductions. Mychelle, who is in her late 30s, told Catherine Francis how they had met. "There were lots of single people in my church but most of them were younger than me and although I socialized with them, I realized I wasn't going to find a partner there. I met plenty of people outside the church but I didn't want a relationship with a non-believer. I felt I needed to enlarge my circle of Christian friends.

"My sister saw an advert for The Network and suggested I try it. The first event I went to was a 20s-and-30s weekend. I arrived full of trepidation, wondering what to expect, but I had a wonderful time. I discovered there were plenty of people in my position and I made lots of good friends from around the country. The events included plenty of activities to enjoy, as well as worship times and some helpful workshops dealing with issues of singleness and the Christian life. The people who run The Network are trained Relate counsellors, so they know what they are doing.

"I'd been a member of The Network for about 18 months when I met Mike, who is the same age as me and lived just fifteen miles away. Initially we began writing to each other and would meet up occasionally with mutual friends and at Network events. There wasn't an immediate attraction – we just got on really well. Over time, our friendship developed into something very special. We got married 18 months later!

"I'd definitely recommend The Network to single Christians. Even if you're not looking for a partner, you can enjoy yourself, meet other people in your position and make friends to socialize or go on holiday with. I really value the friends I made – both male and female – and their support helped me enormously as a single Christian. Finding someone to love was a bonus."

Events do not always flow so smoothly and sometimes more than one introduction is needed before the right person is found. The article goes on to mention single mum Ruth-Naomi, who met her second husband, Peter, through a dating agency. She says, "I was living in Essex with my kids and attending a big church in London. I was keen to marry again but hadn't met anyone at church who was right for me. So when a friend told me about New Day Introductions I got in touch straight away.

"I prayed that the Lord would direct the staff to find the right man for me, and they were praying too. With the first man I met, I knew immediately that he wasn't right for me. Then, a month after joining, I was introduced to Peter, who lived in Wiltshire. He'd also been a member of New Day for about a month and had met one other lady but knew she wasn't the one for him.

"When Peter and I met, it was different from our previous dates. As soon as we started chatting, I felt a great peace. He was easy to talk to, very open and natural. He's a sharing person, which was what I wanted in a husband, and he is on fire for the Lord.

"I was impressed by how well Peter got on with my three

children. He had a daughter himself, from his former marriage, and I'd invited him to bring her along. He ended up playing with all the kids in the garden! It was important for me to find someone who would show love to my children as well as to me." Peter and Ruth-Naomi are now happily married.

Some Christian dating agencies, like the one referred to earlier by Mychelle, arrange events and holidays for singles as well as introducing people with a view to marriage. Last Sunday Richard was preaching at a church in Bromley, Kent. I went with him to the service and afterwards chatted during the coffee-time with David and Jane, a couple who had met through a Christian organization like this. In Jane's church there were no other single people of her age with whom she could be friends or socialize, so she joined the Christian Friendship Fellowship (telephone number: 01302 711007), which introduces people to one another at singles events in local groups, as well as organizing holidays and house parties. She attended several of these and made friends, one of whom was David, who is now her husband. David and Jane are understandably enthusiastic about the organization! CFF will set up penfriendships for those who want them (they have a music-lovers' section, too!) and also provide an introductions service for those who are looking for a marriage partner.

A similar organization is The Network, mentioned earlier by Mychelle. Their telephone number is 01271 817093 and they cater for single, divorced and widowed Christians, providing holidays, weekends and day events. They will also provide personal introductions for those seeking a partner.

Most dating agencies give their details in magazines like *Woman Alive* or *Christianity & Renewal*, which are available in Christian bookshops. Some, like the Beulah Friendship Bureau, which has been in existence for a number of years, provide biblically based suggestions for establishing a successful relationship, as well as guidelines for the introductory meeting. Dating agencies are careful to stress that a first meeting with someone should be in a public venue, such as a restaurant or a pub, that you should make the initial meeting a drink or a brief meal together, and that you should let someone know where you are going. It is best not to give the other person your address at the first meeting.

Christian dating agency fees vary a great deal. Some are as low as £40 and some are above £200 plus VAT. The agencies vary in what they provide for the fee paid. Some guarantee a certain number of introductions within the year's membership registration. Some will provide one-to-one interviews. Some have internet websites. It is a good idea to find out all you can about an agency before registering, so that you know it is run with integrity and you can be happy with its methods.

Some agencies will only take clients up to the age of 45. This includes Choices, the new dating agency run by Ian Gregory, author of *No Sex Please, We're Single* (Kingsway, 2002). The email address is Choices@SimpleIdeas.net. This agency caters for professional people between the ages of 25 and 45 and believes strongly that intellectual compatibility is an important factor in a relationship. Agencies who also cater for older people make it clear that introductions may take longer, especially for older women, as there is such a differential between the number of men and the number of women.

On the internet

The internet is an amazing resource for meeting people in your own country and abroad. Many dating agencies have their own websites, which can take your details and match them with potential partners online; in addition to this, there are websites which simply allow you to contact and make friends with other Christians. As with all internet use, you need to have discernment when "surfing" – you may come across some interesting but unhelpful sites in your search. You may already have a website address, perhaps from a Christian magazine. If so, all you need to do is type it into your browser. Three websites you may find useful are www.ukcmp.org.uk, www.christian-2-christian.co.uk and www.marriageintroductions.co.uk. These agencies are based in the UK. An international site which you may wish to explore is www.christian-dating.com, and you can visit other international and UK sites by using a search engine such as Google (my favourite), Yahoo or Alta Vista, and keying in words and phrases which will give you a result. Suitable keywords are "Christian dating agencies", "Christian marriage partners", and "Christian marriages". There are many more if you have the time and energy!

Singles groups in churches

Many churches have singles groups and they can be useful for bringing single people together in order to socialize and serve. A group like this can help new people coming into the church to get to know a larger number of folk than they would by going through a commitment class into a cell-group or house-group of only a dozen or so people. If the singles group can involve itself in serving each other and the church, and has a strong core membership of keen and committed Christians, it can be a real power in helping those who may come into the church feeling alone and rootless. There can be accountability and care, the addressing of "single" issues, prayer together and an outgoing welcome to new people who tentatively start to attend. It can be a way in to the church family for those who come to church on their own but are too shy to relate easily. The friendship and interaction of a singles group can be what tips the balance and causes people who feel shy and alienated to continue coming to church.

Leaders of church singles groups need to make sure that cliques and exclusive friendships do not cause new people to feel rejected or unwelcome. Also, the group needs to relate to the church as a whole, not just the singles; it's important to keep the church leaders aware of your activities. Sunday school teaching and children's work, helping with refreshments after the service, music ministry and "keeping an eye open" for people on their own are all ways of getting to know others and building friendships. A caring singles group with a strong foundation in its local church can be a good growth factor in the lives of those who belong to it. If the group only meets to socialize, it will probably not have the same impact.

Dating non-Christians

As time goes by, do you find yourself tempted to get involved with a man, *any* man, just to prove to yourself that you aren't that unattractive, even if none of the men at your church seem to be interested? (You've attended Bible Weeks and Christian Growth seminars, but even there the men all seem to be attached or uninterested.) The birthdays tick by, and you begin to wonder whether your longed-for Christian husband will ever materialize. There is Jeremy at work, who is a kind and unselfish man, though he cheerfully admits to being a "convinced unbe-

liever" when you try to witness to him. He is friendly and interested in you and has asked you out several times, though you
have never accepted his invitations – you've always had something on at church, and anyway he isn't a Christian so you don't
want to get involved. But now he begins to seem increasingly
attractive. After all, God hasn't brought a Christian man into
your life and you can't hang on for ever, can you? Maybe if you
go out with him he will come to church, become a Christian,
and he and you will be happy ever after. . . .

Some Christians become romantically involved with unbelievers because they genuinely believe that they can win them
to Christ. If a man is attracted to a Christian woman he may
often be sympathetic towards her church attendance and will
even come to services and meetings with her. All of this raises
her hopes, particularly if she can get her house-group or cell-
group praying for him and inviting him along to social
evenings and group meals. But if she becomes deeply involved
with him and realizes she has allowed herself to fall in love, she
is faced with a choice. She can marry him and continue to
hope that he will come to Christ, or she can take the painful
step of ending the relationship.

Among my friends are those who have taken each of these
courses of action. Some have married their non-Christian
boyfriends, recognizing that they will be in an "unequal
yoke", but continuing to hope and pray for their conversion
to Christ, though this is a very rare occurrence. More usually,
the wife will continue to attend church but her husband will
cease to accompany her. He can hardly be blamed for this, if
his main reason for coming to church was to please his girlfriend! Now that she is his wife he has other opportunities to
please her and be in her company; he sees no reason to go to

church with her. He understands that church is important to her and that she wants to be there on Sundays, just as he wants to play golf or football. But it's not his scene, and he knows she understands that. He gets on well with her friends at church when he sees them, and of course he'll go to a service at Christmas (and at Easter too, if she wants). But he's uncomfortable with too much talk about God and Jesus.

This situation presents some difficult dilemmas and often results in his wife attending church less and even drifting away from God. It's all too much of an effort, particularly when children come along. Does Mummy take them to church with her or do they stay at home with Daddy? Do we go to the beach on Sunday as a family or do we only go to the park because we have to wait for Mummy to come home from church? There is the added heartache of knowing that you and your partner are living as husband and wife and yet are not united in Christ. You can't pray together, worship together, share truth together or live by the same standards. You are following Jesus; he isn't. (We will look at this situation again in the subsequent chapters.)

Some women make the choice to break with a boyfriend who makes it clear that he is not interested in becoming a Christian. This can be enormously painful, especially if the relationship has been a long one with a great deal of emotional commitment. The boyfriend may be very upset and bewildered, unable to see quite why his girlfriend no longer wants to continue their relationship. He's been happy for her to go to church on Sundays and see her Christian friends. He hasn't pressured her to sleep with him – or only once or twice at the beginning, before she made it clear that as a Christian she believed sex was only for marriage; he had respected that, although it had been difficult for him. But they'd had some great times together and he'd thought they were going to make it "up the aisle". So why this change on her part?

It may be very difficult for the Christian girl to communicate to her boyfriend her reasons for ending the relationship. All she can do is be honest with him and trust God to help him understand. The recognition that her faith means so much to her may help him to realize that Christianity is worth exploring.

And will a Christian boyfriend now appear on the scene? It's possible to feel that now you have honoured God in giving up an unequal relationship, God will send you a tall, handsome, godly boyfriend in double-quick time! But God does not think like we do (Isaiah 55:8) and he is never in a hurry. He wants us to learn from the choices we make and to grow as a result of them. Can you learn to trust him for your future relationships?

Older singles

Older single women may find themselves battling against the "if onlys" of life. "If only I had had a husband", "If only I'd had children", "If only I had someone special to love me" – "my life would be so different!" Dwelling constantly on this makes fertile soil for resentment and bitterness.

Many older single women are faced with caring for ageing parents who will become increasingly dependent. Facing an uncertain financial future alone is another burden in these days of economic uncertainty and job impermanence, even if a satisfying career is the reality at present. And how can a single woman (especially if she is still living with her parents) become emotionally mature? Many single women move away from the family home for work or marriage within a few years of ending their education; if they have been to college or university they have been used to living apart from their parents even before that. But for a single woman continuing to live at home, particularly if she is the only child, there must be a separation of her identity from that of her parents; her accommodation in the home needs to give her independence and freedom of movement so that she is able to grow as an individual, entertaining her own friends and leading her own life as well as having involvement with her parents.

A positive approach

My friend Angela is a lively and attractive woman in her 50s. She is a former teacher and was a missionary in Nigeria for twelve years. She now works for a Christian organization which seeks to befriend international students at colleges and universities in Britain. She arranges social activities and events for them and shares the good news of the gospel of Jesus Christ when there are opportunities to do so. She relies on the help and co-operation of local churches of all denominations; she herself has an ever-open home to which she welcomes anyone who needs a cup of tea, a shoulder to cry on or a Long Talk About Life!

Visiting Angela is often like walking into a United Nations conference – students from China, Singapore, South Korea, Egypt, Denmark and other far-away places find their way to her home. Bible studies in her London flat helped their English as well as being an introduction for those who wanted to know about Christianity, and a place of warm fellowship for those who were already Christians.

Angela has now relocated to East Anglia and is working with students there. She has bought a house and is settling into the area, where she knew nobody at first. All she had were some introductions to local churches. She admitted that the house-move had underlined her singleness to her. "Leaving London was such a big decision to make," she said. "It was clearly what God was leading me to do, and the leaders in my organization agreed with my decision. But I had to make the move alone. My choice would have been to have a husband – but God provided lots of practical and financial support from friends when I needed it. They were a wonderful help with hanging curtains, painting, drilling and all those other things you have to do when you move house!"

I asked Angela if she had expected to marry. "Yes, I think everybody expects to marry," she said. "It wasn't an expectation from my parents; it was a natural desire. But I didn't meet anyone I wanted to marry, and I was teaching in Africa from the age of 28 until I came back to England at 40. I had been thinking and praying about returning permanently to the UK and then my dad became ill, which confirmed to me that I should come back to be near my parents. Later, when I began working among students, I still expected to marry, and it is something I pray about occasionally even now." She grinned. "I'd like a nice widower with children! To be honest, it was when I returned to Nigeria after my first three-month home assignment in England that the fact that I was alone really hit me and I began to say to God that unless I married I would not want to come back to Nigeria again – it was too hard. In Nigeria all respectable women are married, and a single woman working in a Muslim culture is a bit of an anomaly. So I told God definitely that I didn't want to come back again without a husband. But he didn't bring me one. Instead he spoke to me clearly from Matthew's gospel, 'Take my yoke upon you and learn from me.' I knew I was yoked with him and that enabled me to go back on my own again. I felt that as I had given my life to the Lord that was where he wanted me, single, at that time. But it wasn't easy – what I accepted in my head didn't always fit in with my heart!"

I asked Angela about the particular problems and pressures of her single situation. Did she find it difficult living alone? (Even though her spare room is frequently occupied!) "The house feels different when there's someone else in it as well as me," she admitted thoughtfully. "I don't like being alone for too long. I'm aware that I always fill up my Saturdays well in advance – I can't bear to be on my own at weekends. Holidays are another biggie. I wouldn't go away on my own, though I know lots of people do. But I'm grateful to God that he has always provided someone to go with, or to stay with. I'm a 'type E' personality on the Myers–Briggs scale, so to function well I need people with me!"

Anything else? "I think the whole 'image' thing can be a problem for older single women – the media so often portrays them as frumpy or eccentric. You need a good younger friend or two to tell you if your clothes and appearance are OK. (I guess daughters do it for married women!) Because I'm working with students I have to look right – some of them see me as a role model."

I asked her how she felt about the matter of children. "Well, I recognize that physically it's too late to have my own. When the realization of that hit me, I knew I had to trust God to enable me to cope with it. And a lot of my friends are now talking to me about their grandchildren, so I realize I'm missing out on grandmothering as well. But I like children, and I get on well with them. I have two nieces of my own, and I enjoy other people's children, too. Churches should encourage people with children to share them with single people – it could be mutually beneficial!"

Had there been other, long-term pressures? "Yes – hopes that aren't realized. I've travelled a lot, and each time I went into a new situation people would say, "This is where you'll meet the man of your dreams!" And it never happened. Over the years this gets painful, especially when you really want to meet someone and you don't. It's as if you are holding a bunch of balloons, and every time you are disappointed another balloon is popped. Mind you, it has often been other people's expectations that have influenced me to hope that this time or this place will be where it will all happen.

"I'm not single by choice, but by circumstance, and I think this applies to many single women. If the right man came along, they would marry. I would love God to bring a husband into my life, and that may still happen.

"I do sometimes wonder," she said soberly, "what I would do if I were tempted to marry someone who was not a Christian. That isn't something I have been faced with, but I know people who have had to make that decision. I do have bad days, but I'm trusting God that my present situation is his best for me right now, and I recognize that I need to be content, rather than becoming bitter that God, at this moment, hasn't given me what I want. He is my firm foundation, and he has given me good friends and family." She smiled. "One last word. The church generally labels us 'singles'. We're not 'singles' – we're people!"

Is late marriage right for you?

Whether or not to marry in later life is a decision which needs prayerful consideration. Is this the right thing to do, simply because the person and the opportunity are there? You need to think carefully about what you will lose, as well as what you will gain. Yes, you will have a husband! But you will have to alter your life to accommodate him, just as he will to accommodate you. If you both have homes you will have to decide which one you will live in, or whether to sell both of them and look for somewhere new. If you decide to live in yours, or even in somewhere new, will you be able to lose space happily to all "his" stuff? This does not just mean clothes, furniture and kitchen gear, but books, compact discs, fitness equipment, fishing rods or other hobby paraphernalia which he has collected over the years. Will the stuff of his life mesh happily with yours? (Not only material goods, but the routines, the likes and dislikes, the friends, the finance, the families!) You have been independent for a long time. Are you prepared to lose your freedom in terms of time, use of money, holiday plans, even the hour at which you eat dinner in the evening?

Marrying in later life involves more adjustment and compromise than younger couples face, to say nothing of self-sacrifice and commitment! There should be as much preparation for it as possible, and an honest recognition from both sides about what is involved. You may feel that you are too "mature" for your church's "marriage preparation" course, but do it anyway!

Don't marry for the sake of a wedding ring and a new name, or because "he's asked me, so it must be right". But if you truly love him, and he loves you, and you are going into marriage realistically, prepared to accommodate each other and having your eyes wide open, you can make it work. After all, if he's been cooking in his bachelor kitchen all these years he must know what's what with a blender and a food processor, so you could be on the brink of a whole new life in more ways than you think.

Becoming single again

Every woman on the planet experiences singleness. Some leave their single situation early on in life, others much later. Some remain single for their lifetime. Because women live longer than men, singleness is a state to which many married women return through widowhood. Some return to singleness through divorce. Divorce rates in England are the second highest in Europe. If the present trend continues, 40% of new marriages will eventually reach the divorce courts. Christians are not immune to this, and many Christian wives have had to divorce husbands who, despite their Christian profession, have violated their marriage vows and damaged their families through adultery, addiction and physical or psychological abuse. If a husband in this kind of situation refuses to change or to seek help, and if children are at risk, a wife sometimes has little alternative but to divorce him.

Single through divorce

"Divorce is painful – people who do it should know before they start how painful it is," said my friend Rosemary, who is in her late 40s. The pain and shock of divorce came unexpectedly to her nine years ago. Brad, her husband, had always been a flirt, but because they were both committed Christians she felt she could trust him. Their daughter, Rebecca, was a toddler when Brad, who was an accountant, had an affair with a woman he met on a course connected with his work. He eventually confessed to Rosemary, who was devastated by his betrayal. She pleaded with him to end his excessive flirting with other women, but he would not, and his behaviour towards Rosemary became more and more uncaring. By now their younger daughter Lucy had been born, and life became difficult, as the unhappy and tense atmosphere in their home affected the children.

"My problem is that I am a very independent person," Rosemary admitted. "I didn't want to tell anyone what was going on or ask for help. Eventually I did talk to our pastor, and he spent a lot of time over several years trying to help us. We were actually leading a house-group in the church until a year before we divorced. But I couldn't carry on with that; I felt that it was hypocritical to be leading a group when our relationship was coming apart. Outwardly I appeared to be coping with the situation, but inwardly I got to a point where I was considering suicide.

"Our pastor continued to talk with us both, but Brad would neither repent nor change his behaviour, and I knew our marriage would have to end, even though divorce was against everything I believed, as I had taken my marriage vows very seriously. I told him I was going to see a solicitor, and he became upset and promised me that things would be different, so I agreed to wait three months. But nothing changed. One of the worst things for me was that all through this time Brad continued coming to church and worshipping with great enthusiasm, in spite of the fact that he was betraying me and breaking up our marriage.

"I went ahead with the divorce, and I knew that I had done the right thing. Through every stage of it I asked God for his guidance and help, and I asked him to stop me if I should not go through with it. Just before I sent in the forms for the decree absolute, Brad became seriously involved with yet another woman. His behaviour and the effect it had on me and the children made me realize that the divorce was necessary and right.

"Later, I had some sessions with a counsellor who was very helpful to me and enabled me to see that Brad's behaviour indicated great emotional immaturity and that in fact he was still very dependent on his mother emotionally, and had never 'cut the apron strings'. Understanding this helped me to come to a place of forgiveness, though it didn't ease the pain, because I did love him very much.

"I had realized that something was wrong when Rebecca was very ill at fifteen months old. The hospital suspected that she had meningitis, and warned me that she might not survive the night. Brad stayed away the whole time – he did not give me any support at all. When Lucy was born I had severe post-natal depression; he could not cope with that, and told me while I was going through it that he did not love me. I realized that he could not deal with crises in an adult fashion. He would never meet my needs, only his own.

"When we split up, he did not give me any financial support for three months; I think it was his way of trying to get me back. He thought if I had no money I would have to go back to him. Thankfully, my parents were able to help us, and I had a teaching job three days a week. But we had to move out of our house into a tiny flat which the children hated. Eventually, we were able to rent a house which was owned by a friend who was moving out of the area – she charged me the same rent as I had been paying at the flat! Then, a year or two later, I was able to buy the house. God has been so good to me, and I know that I have learned to trust him to meet my needs in a way I could never have imagined.

"Since the divorce my life has changed. My faith in God has grown as I've seen him answer prayer. My self-image is much stronger now. During my marriage Brad would continually put me down, and I knew that my thoughts and opinions would be brushed aside. Now I'm more confident. It's been hard bringing up the girls on my own but we have had lots of support from our church and they have grown up well. Both of them love the Lord and enjoy being part of the church.

"When things first began to go wrong, I was angry with God. If God is for marriage, why wasn't mine working, especially as we were both Christians? I found it difficult to worship and pray, and I felt that God didn't love me. But when we finally divorced, I found it much easier to trust God. In spite of all the financial problems and the effect of the divorce, life became better. The children stopped wetting the bed, and gradually life became more settled and normal for them. They were ten and seven when we divorced, and Rebecca became very withdrawn for several months. Lucy had tantrums which were clearly for the purpose of seeing whether I would be as firm with them now that I was on my own!

"They are growing up now, and I am free to go out more. One day I would like to remarry but I don't think the time is right yet. I'm a full-time teacher, and I have seen the problems that some children have when step-parents are introduced into their families. When the girls are older I'll be open to God bringing someone else into my life. I prayed that God would make me content with my single life, and he has done that. Brad has married again; the girls see him every week. At times it has been awkward, for instance at Rebecca's baptism three years ago – she wanted both of us there, and both sets of grandparents too, though Brad's mother was refusing to speak to me at the time! Brad and I had made an agreement that we would not talk badly about each other to the girls, and we have respected that. They have accepted his new wife as a friend, and it is not so difficult now to be there together for the children's events.

"My big regret is that I haven't had the experience of a happy marriage or of being special to my husband in the way I believed I would be because we were both Christians. Yes, I feel I've been robbed of that. But I have been able to forgive Brad, and I have experienced God's love and provision. I can trust him for the future."

Sue Ashdown's brilliant book *Till Death Us Do Part?* (published by Eagle, 1998, £5.99) describes her experience of a marriage which broke down not once, but twice. Her husband, who was vicar of the parish where she lived, left her and their two school-age daughters to live with a woman parishioner with whom he had been having an affair. Sue and her daughters had to move out of their church-owned house and begin a new life in a new area; they could not remain near the church where her husband had been the vicar. As well as losing her friends through the move, she had to help her two girls cope with the loss of their father; she also had to take on a full-time job to support the three of them.

After two years her husband returned, assuring her he would never leave her again. They retook their marriage vows in a ceremony with the bishop, and eventually her husband was reinstated in his ministry, assisting at the church they were attending and eventually becoming vicar of a daughter church. The family moved back into a church house, and soon their two daughters left school to begin nursing careers in London. Sue and her husband continued with their ministry, enjoying their friendship with the rector of the main parish church and his wife; as far as Sue was concerned, life was fulfilling and satisfying.

Some months later she began to suspect that something was wrong in her relationship with her husband, but nothing prepared her for the revelation, in a letter just before Christmas, that her husband had been having an affair for 18 years with a woman in the north of England, where he had been a parish priest in the early years of their marriage. This was a different woman from the one he had left her to live with a few years before. Her letter asked Sue to "give him up or, if you can't do that, share him", and went on to state that they would continue the relationship anyway. Shaking uncontrollably, Sue confronted her husband with the letter which she knew meant the end of their marriage.

The following months were unspeakably painful for Sue. "Telling my daughters was excruciating. I met them at the nurses' home in London. My stepmother came with me to help me, for I have only one pair of arms and I knew that on that day I would need two."

Sue found herself packing to leave a church house for the second time in her life. She went to stay with her sister while she took stock of her life. Her grief and pain caused her to feel as if she were drowning: "I felt truly like I imagine a drowning person feels. For a start, this time I was truly alone. The girls were both nursing in London. I had no home, no church, no money, no job, no role, no town, no identity and no husband."

She felt guilty at first about her strong feelings of hatred and anger toward the woman who had taken her husband, and about her own fear, doubt and despair, but says she has learned that as Christians we are not immune to any human emotion – it is what we do with those emotions that matters. In the depths of her pain Sue held on to God, believing and trusting that he was still in control of her life and that he cared deeply for her and for her daughters, whom she had not been able to protect from the results of their father's actions. She has plumbed the depths of rejection, grief and hurt, and has written, five years on, a book full of wisdom and strength for those going through the experiences of betrayal, separation and divorce.

"I sometimes think how amazing it is," she writes, "that something we find out in one day can change our whole lives, including our perception of ourselves. It may well have been going on for years, but for all of us there is that certain moment in time when we finally know. And in that moment is born the beginning of frighteningly deep feelings and pain about ourselves. Obviously, I cannot speak for other people. All I can say for myself is that it will take many years for the scars to heal – and it may not be until I meet my God face to face. There are still many times when I feel the effects of being betrayed and rejected. I still 'take offence' far too easily. I feel 'left out' of things very quickly, and then feel extremely stupid when it becomes obvious there was a valid reason for it. I know others will be able to identify with my feelings of lack of self-confidence, over-sensitivity to criticism, and sometimes, even now, pure shame. Not shame for myself, but for the effect of what has happened on so many other people. And for the shame it has brought on the church of God, and sometimes, I think, on the very name of God himself."

Sue goes on to write about her experience of God's love holding her during the very bad times. She encourages any Christian woman enduring the agony of divorce and grieving over the loss of her shared life, to recognize that God is with her and for her, and understands her pain.

"If you remember nothing else, remember this. When Jesus hung on the cross, he faced the ultimate betrayal and rejection, by his friends, by his race, and worst of all, by his heavenly Father. God is part of Christ, and Christ is part of God – and there was this terrible separation. Separated from part of himself – rejected by part of himself. There can be no greater betrayal than this, and we can never experience anything a fraction as devastating. So not only has Christ suffered in all ways as we do, but he has suffered a hundred thousand times more. He has been all the way – and beyond, for us – for you. Maybe we feel too bad to pray or go to church. Maybe the very last thing we want to do is to mix with a load of other Christians! Don't worry, that's OK. But if we can just hold on to the fact that he is there, then he will hold on to us and never let us go."

In one chapter Sue suggests ways of dealing with episodes of anger and pain, such as weeping with a trusted friend, or doing something physical and energetic when anger threatens to overwhelm you. For her, writing proved to be the way to release her deepest feelings, and several of her powerful poems are included in the book. Her final chapters deal with acceptance of the situation, without which it is impossible to reach a place of forgiveness or to move on into the next phase of life.

As she says, "I wanted so much to have it all back, to be back in the past with the husband I love and for the past to be *now*. But I found that as I tried to build a new life, at the same time I had to find a way to stop doing that. It is impossible to walk forward when our heads are screwed round looking back over our shoulders."

She stresses that time is needed to come to terms with all that has been lost and why God allowed it to happen, pointing out the need to recognize that God gives us freedom of choice, and in that freedom we often hurt one another. Where there are no answers we have to live with the questions. Counselling can be helpful, both in helping us deal with what has happened and in helping us learn to know the new person we will become.

I thoroughly recommend Sue Ashdown's book and also *Single Again* by Jim Smoke (Gazelle Books, now Monarch Books, 2000, £6.99). Jim has run "divorce recovery" groups in the United States for many years, and is a gifted singles' counsellor. His book contains much wisdom for those who are learning to live as an individual again rather than part of a couple. There are helpful chapters on sexuality, coping with the loss of friends, reading the Bible and keeping on track spiritually, redefining your identity, finding a support system, taking responsibility for health and fitness and looking to the future. There is a useful section for single parents and a chapter on remarriage.

Help agencies

Sue Ashdown lists several help agencies in the back of her book, including the Samaritans, Relate and Families Need Fathers. There is another organization active in the UK called

DivorceCare, which is based in London, though the main office is in the United States. DivorceCare works with churches to provide help and counsel for those going through divorce. Church ministers and leaders are supplied with excellent materials and shown how to train leaders of groups which will provide ongoing care and emotional support in a loving Christian environment. Support for groups is constantly available from DivorceCare headquarters. The telephone number for this helpful organization is 020 8534 7339.

Single through bereavement

Some women become single again in a moment through the unexpected death of their partner. I wrote in chapter 2 about the air crash which killed the five friends of Dr James Dobson. Whether it happens through an accident or a sudden illness, the shock and trauma can be powerful.

Geoff, my friend Karen's husband, died from a pulmonary embolism on his way home from a business trip. He was 36 years old. He and Karen had been on holiday with their two children and several friends a fortnight before, and there had been no warning of what was about to happen. Geoff had been fit and healthy, swimming and playing golf, having fun with his children. He had been a little breathless now and then but did not think anything of it, as he was having a very active holiday and knew he was slightly overweight.

Immediately after their holiday, Geoff left for a week's business trip in France. He felt unwell towards the end of the week away, but decided, rather than seeing a French doctor, to wait and see his own doctor on his return. But he was taken ill in his car when he left the ferry at Folkestone and by the time the ambulance reached the hospital with him he was dead. Karen, who was happily preparing for his return, received a terrible shock when the hospital telephoned her with the news. Her pastor drove her to the hospital, 60 miles away, and helped her through the dreadful hours that followed, as she broke the news to eight-year-old Stephanie and ten-year-old Jack that their daddy would not be coming home to them. Her mother drove up from Wiltshire to stay with her, and her friends and church family supported her and the children through the funeral and the subsequent grief-stricken weeks.

I spoke to Karen two months after Geoff's death. It was just before Christmas and the pain in her eyes was evident as she talked about him. "Suddenly I feel as if I have no future," she said. "It was so clear before, but now I'm just living day by day. I know God is with me and helping me, though I was very angry with him for letting this happen. At first I wanted to die – I was tempted to go to bed cuddling Geoff's shirt and swallow loads of pills. But the thought of the children pulled me back, and I know that suicide is wrong.

"The children and I are all sleeping together at night – that way we can comfort each other. Stephanie talks about how Daddy would cuddle her if she woke up in the night, and Jack talks about how he and his dad used to do arm-wrestling – then Stephanie gets upset and tells him not to talk about it! She was very upset that Daddy wouldn't see her Christmas show at school. Christmas is going to be hard, but the worst thing is knowing that Geoff won't be part of the year 2000. Everyone else is getting excited about the millennium but I just can't when he's not here."

Geoff's funeral had been a wonderful testimony. He and Karen had only been Christians for four years and in that time Geoff had grown in his knowledge of God, enjoyed being part of the church, and had witnessed about his new-found faith in Jesus. Many of his unconverted friends and work colleagues came to his funeral and heard people testify to the influence Geoff had had on their lives. Several spoke about his very evident love for his wife and children, and others talked about the way his friendship had helped them. His pastor went on to preach the gospel; several people came to faith in Jesus as a result of that funeral, including Geoff's brother-in-law. Karen is glad about this and deeply appreciative of the help and support she received on that day, but she would rather have her husband back than know that people were blessed by his funeral.

I talked to Karen again eight months after Geoff's death. "I know I'm a different person now," she admitted. "When you go through this experience, another person comes out at the other end. I'm living a different kind of life, even though everything around me is the same. I'm still a mum and I have to keep life going on as usual for the kids. At school their teachers have been really good with them, and they chat about Geoff more easily now. They have lots of happy memories of him. At first, lots of friends were willing to step in for their dad and do things with them – but obviously everyone has their own lives and that kind of support can't carry on indefinitely.

"I've had to learn to do lots of things that Geoff used to do for me. For instance, he would never let me drive on a motorway! I wasn't a very independent person – I never had to be. Now I'm having to discover myself as an individual. After Geoff died I lost all my confidence; I seemed to be living in an alien world. Even the street and my garden seemed strange and different – it was scary. The grief and anger have been terrible, and at first I didn't want the children's love, although I knew they needed me. It wasn't the children I wanted, it was Geoff, and it was terrible that I couldn't be cuddled or held by him. Now I am able to give them that love – and we all find ourselves very much in need of love and cuddles.

"I can carry on normally, but the grief doesn't go away. It catches me unexpectedly at different times when I hear a song or something that reminds me of Geoff. I find it difficult in church not to be reduced to tears, yet I know I need the support of my brothers and sisters in the Lord and I know I want to be where people are worshipping him. But I miss Geoff so much – at first I found it very hard to get out of bed in the mornings. If it hadn't been for the children I would have just pulled the covers over my head and slept all day. I'm not so bad now, though – it has improved. Being able to talk about him has helped. I haven't kept everything bottled up inside; I've been able to talk to friends and tell people how I feel."

For Karen, bereavement has not only made her single again, it has made her a single parent, and she feels her responsibility to help and care for Jack and Stephanie in their loss of their daddy, while at the same time coping with her own grief and sadness. She feels that in some ways losing a partner through death is different from losing a partner through divorce; the results and the difficulties may be the same, but the memories do not have the same power to cause hurt and rejection. There are no constant reminders, through the children's visits, of the former partner and the person with whom he is now living.

For the majority of women, widowhood is experienced later in life. But whatever our age, widowhood, like divorce, is an unwelcome new life. We do not go willingly through the door and we adjust with difficulty and pain to life on the other side of it. Like Karen, we may feel that we are different people now. Coming through grief to an acceptance of God's will, even though we do not understand it (Proverbs 20:24) and would not have wanted it, can help us to begin facing life again. God's promises are true and his word is reliable. He will be with you in the emotional upheaval of your grief and anger and as you walk in the new opportunities of your "different" life. He will help you as you bring up your children and seek to make their lives secure and peaceful. He will be with you as you face the birthdays and Christmases, the anniversaries and the parents' evenings alone. He will send people who can help you sort out finances and house problems. Let your church help you, and go to your church leaders if you are in difficulties. But above all, put your trust in Jesus and let him comfort you. If you are finding it hard to concentrate, stay in one Bible passage and just read a verse or two of it each day, receiving it as God's word to you. Psalm 42, Psalm 91, John 14, Romans 8:28–39 and Ephesians 1:1–14 are all helpful passages.

I am aware, as I write, that I have not personally been through the "doors" of widowhood or divorce, and that I did not have a long experience of single life. But I have proved the truth of God's word in times of severe trial and difficulty, and I know he will be as faithful in your life as he has been in mine.

Facing the future

You may feel that life is just too difficult and that your present situation of singleness, whatever the reason for it, heralds an empty future and possibly a lonely old age with no husband to care whether it's your birthday or not and no wedding anniversaries to celebrate. Singleness can be a hurt which does not go away, in spite of a loving support network of friends and a good church. But God is the God of hope, and he does not want you to be locked into resentment or bitterness. He wants to heal your hurt and fill your life with his love and peace, he wants your arms to be open to others who are hurting. He wants to speak to you as an individual about his love for you and about his plans and purposes for your life. Whether you are single, divorced or bereaved he cares deeply for you, his beloved child; he has a ministry and a task for you, and he wants you to grow in your love and knowledge of him, in honest fellowship and unity with his people and free from envy and unfulfilled longing.

At the end of John's gospel we read about Peter taking a walk with Jesus to discuss his own future ministry (John 21). Peter looks over his shoulder and sees John following them. "Lord, what about him?" he says. Jesus replies, "If I want him to remain alive until I return, what is that to you? You must follow me" (John 21:21–22).

To consider: Are you living in resentment or contentment?

Is there some positive action you can take right now (eg approach someone about planning a holiday, make a strategy list, invite someone to breakfast, register with a Christian dating agency)?

Have you had an inappropriate and unrealistic view of marriage? If this is the case, are there areas of your life which need God's healing?

Are you separated, divorced or bereaved? At what stage are you in terms of healing, recovery and moving on? Are you aware of God's comfort and care? Do you need to seek the help of a Christian counsellor?

CHAPTER FOUR

SEASONS OF MARRIAGE

The marriage season can take us through all kinds of weather, from spring sunshine to summer heat, by way of snowstorms, thunder and lightning, with dull, overcast days and the odd tornado thrown in. In this chapter we will look at some of the joys and hazards of this season, and look for ways to find calmer weather – or at least an umbrella for the rainshowers!

Many years ago I stood by the motor racing circuit at Brands Hatch. As I listened to the roar of the cars and saw the excitement and enthusiasm of the spectators, I wondered what on earth I was doing there; I had never been remotely interested in racing cars. A couple of weeks later I stood in similar bewilderment on the sidelines of a rugby match at the Old Deer Park in Twickenham. I didn't understand the rules of the game then, and I still don't. The reason for my unlikely presence at these two events was the young man escorting me – a young man who was beginning to fill my thoughts a great deal and who, finding great enjoyment in racing cars and rugby matches, wanted me to enjoy them with him. I never did learn to enjoy either of these pursuits but I did marry the young man, and we found many other things we mutually enjoyed (though he still likes to watch motor racing and rugby!).

We came into our marriage with joy, hope and expectation. We were optimistic – it never occurred to us to be otherwise. So we were unprepared for the problems. Both of us had come from fairly dysfunctional families. Richard's parents had divorced when he was nine (see chapter 2), and his mother brought him to London from the north of England, away from his father and twin brother and sister; all contact with them was lost, and he had to adjust to a new stepfather and, eventually, two younger sisters. He told me, after we had been married for some years, that on several occasions during his teens he had been tempted to take his own life. I had suffered a great deal of verbal abuse from my mother from the time my baby brother was born when I was nearly three. Right through my childhood I was aware that she preferred my brother, and at eight years old I was sent to a convent boarding-school, where I was very unhappy. My mother hoped that the nuns would succeed in improving my unruly behaviour; I don't think it ever occurred to her to link my bad behaviour with her attitude to me!

We both felt that marriage would wipe out all the sorrows of our past, and that in loving one another and being committed to one another and to the Lord who had saved us and given us new life, it had to be all downhill from here on. How wrong we were! Enormous (but unrecognized) rejection problems, lack of role models and little understanding of gender differences in temperament and approach, combined to bring many difficulties into our relationship. Unmet needs and unreal expectations are a lethal combination! Yet we loved each other deeply, and our foundation of faith in God and in the truth of the Scriptures enabled us, over the years, to work at the problems in our lives and our marriage, and to face things as God revealed them.

Expectations and realities

We all come into marriage with certain expectations. These largely depend on our past experiences and the families in which we have grown up. My friend Georgia has a fanatically tidy mother, who cleans the bathroom the instant it is vacated, whisks plates off the table the moment they are cleared and hoovers her house every single day. Her table is laid meticulously for every meal, with the correct silver and napkins. When Georgia married Mike and had her own home, she took great delight in putting the milk bottle on the table without even decanting the milk into a jug, as a celebration of freedom from her mother's compulsively strict housekeeping. (And she only dusts once a week!)

Susie, another friend, has a dad who thoroughly enjoys "do-it-yourself" and makes many things for the home, as well as doing any repairs that are necessary. When she married Terry, she assumed that he would be able to do the same things. She had to come to terms with the fact that her expectations had been unreal; Terry's skills are much more academic than practical. Eventually, with loving encouragement, Terry mastered the basics of painting and paper-hanging. Criticism and derision would not have helped him to acquire these skills, but an attitude of love and acceptance, combined with a determination on Susie's part not to compare his work with her dad's, enabled him to become competent even if not expert.

Reactive expectations are common; if you had a remote and

uncommunicative father you may be subconsciously looking for a husband who will be warm and responsive. If you had a competitive father who always wanted you to do better, climb higher, work harder and produce better results, you may find yourself looking for a partner who is more relaxed in his attitudes and loves you the way you are rather than pushing you to achieve greater heights. An absent father, who had either left the marriage or who was never there for you, can leave you constantly searching for a father's love – and possibly entering an unsuitable relationship because of your need. The reality is that only a deep experience of God's fatherly love, commitment and care can alleviate the pain and emptiness of a missing father; no man can ever do this.

Some of our expectations come from media advertising. We see couples eating a wonderful meal in a beautiful restaurant, or enjoying one another's company while decorating a lovely flat or house. Expectations can be dangerous, especially when the reality proves very different. Wrong attitudes begin with the shortfall between expectation and actuality.

An attitude of resentment

Observing Christian marriages over the years (including my own!), I am convinced that the most damaging factor in a marriage is an attitude of resentment, which can show itself in many different forms. Resentment means "to feel again", and the pain which comes from a husband's hurtful behaviour can be "felt again" many times, and if there is no way it can be talked through together and a solution found or an apology offered, the hurt can take hold in our heart and become a "bitter root" (Hebrews 12:15) which will affect the whole relationship.

Courtship and engagement behaviour does not usually engender reactive resentment; during that time you are both aware of the need to nurture your relationship, therefore thoughtfulness and caring attitudes prevail. Apologies for anything less are readily offered and received. Flowers, love notes, tickets for events, attentive behaviour, long talks, the sharing of your life-stories, your hopes and your dreams – all of these happen during the pre-marriage months, culminating in wedding vows made to each other in words that indicate a future where life will continue in this way, where the man who is now your husband will be your lover, your confidant, your "forever friend", wanting to share his own life, his thoughts and aspirations, his very soul with you for always.

I have thought long and hard about the many couples I have known and whose weddings I have attended, but I cannot think of *any* couple I know where this happy scenario has actually ensued! Marriage, and subsequently parenthood, seems to change a man, and the river of loving communication which is present before the wedding seems to dry up. The caring, understanding guy who looked out for your every need and understood the meaning of your every glance, seems to have disappeared. Tillie, a close friend of mine, experienced an idyllic year of engagement to Bob before their wedding ten years ago. Marriage and the birth of three boys seemed to have ended their deep "togetherness", though they still loved each other.

"I've come to the conclusion," Tillie said to me one day, "that all husbands are the same. They love us, there's no doubt about that, but they certainly don't understand us!" Undoubtedly, it is that lack of understanding, from a partner who promised so much, that can spark the beginnings of a resentful attitude in a wife who feels denied the love and deep communication she had expected from her Christian husband.

How do we handle this, as Christian wives who really desire to walk with God and live like Jesus? Attitudes of disappointment, frustration and anger will not achieve change (though the expression of these emotions may temporarily relieve us). We need to look at the situation honestly and prayerfully, and remind ourselves of two facts: one, marriage is a commitment which has to be worked at, and two, the Holy Spirit's power in a husband's life is what will bring about change, not the urgent expression of our hurt feelings. What are the biblical ground-rules for a Christian couple who want their marriage to be glorifying to God? Recognizing unreal expectations and dealing with resentment are surely two of the most important.

Criticism and comparison

Resentment has many components, and two very powerful ones are *criticism* and *comparison*. These attitudes are not usually present during the early weeks and months of marriage, when the joyful urgency of sex and the novelty of living together and finding a new programme for life takes all our time and energy, especially if you are both working. But later, after the blissful "newly married" months are over, you may find yourself becoming critical of your husband's manner or "style". Perhaps he is very different from you – and that may be what attracted you to him initially. As we saw earlier, we may be unconsciously searching for a husband who is different from our own father. But also we tend to seek out, consciously or unconsciously, partners who have the qualities we lack. This can be a good thing, because two opposite natures can combine to make a well-rounded partnership, but the adjustment into that well-rounded partnership can take much painful time to achieve (well-rounded all too often becomes pear-shaped!).

Resentful thoughts can creep in and spoil your relationship, making it become a "foothold for the devil" (Ephesians 4:27) who is as pleased to spoil a Christian marriage as he is to split a church. What begins as gentle criticism (often referred to as "constructive") can become a damaging attitude which affects you as well as your husband and your relationship. The strong, dependable guy who was your anchor and rock, and whose strength of character delighted you, can become in your eyes a stubborn, overbearing partner who digs his heels in and stands in the way of what you want to do. The easygoing bloke who had such a relaxed approach to life and never worried if you didn't bother about a particular task may begin to drive you crazy by his laid-back attitude to everything, from jobs in the home and garden to disciplining the children. Criticism is often followed by *comparison*. Mentally, and even verbally, you may find yourself comparing him with others and wishing he was more like Clare's Pete, or Liz's Clive. Perhaps you try to cover up for his laziness or lack of punctuality by organizing or nagging him into action.

I remember a time in our own marriage when God showed me very vividly the way I was criticizing Richard in my heart. We had been in the ministry for several years. Both of us had been filled with the Spirit, and the church was growing and moving in God. But at this point in time we were "out of communication", and my attitude had become very critical. Richard had been out most evenings for several weeks, and there were matters concerning the children that I needed to discuss with him. I was feeling hurt at seeing so little of him, and I accused him of going out to solve other people's problems and never being around for the problems in his own family. Richard became quiet and uncommunicative over several days of noisy criticism from me, and the quieter he became the more I tried to goad him into some reaction. I wanted a good argument; it would have made me feel much better to let off steam! But that wasn't the way Richard worked, and somehow this fact made me even more cross. (Looking back later, we realized that we had been under real enemy attack; God was moving powerfully in the church, and people were being changed. The devil does not relinquish ground without a fight, and leaders are often the first target of his attack. He obviously reasoned that if he could destroy our relationship Richard's teaching and preaching on the power and work of the Holy Spirit would lose all credibility.)

One day I went to our bedroom and began to pray in desperation for God to break in and show us some answers. As I was praying, God showed me a vivid picture. In my mind I could see a beautiful tropical beach with deep blue sea, palm trees and acres of golden sand stretching for miles. In the middle of this wonderful beach I could see a small, black pebble. Then someone came running across the wide expanse of sand. As I watched, the figure tripped over the black pebble and fell flat on its face. Then God's voice spoke in my heart: *"That figure is you. The beach is Richard. Instead of appreciating what I have given you in Richard, all his love and integrity, you are majoring on one aspect of his character that you don't like, and you are allowing that to affect your whole relationship."* Following this revelation, I knew that repentance was in order – for me, not Richard.

Criticism, nagging and manipulation will never change your husband; it may even be counter-productive. Only a change in his own heart will produce a change in his behaviour. Attempting to change your husband through your efforts from the outside may actually prevent God reaching him to change his heart and motivation from the inside. It will also militate against the development or re-establishment of loving communication between you. Your husband will not feel secure in your love if he is aware that you are constantly trying to change him. The only message that comes through is, "She doesn't like what I am", inevitably followed by, "Why did she marry me, then?" No man can learn to take responsibility for his actions when his wife treats him as a child, "organizing" his time and arrangements. Neither will he be able to take any lead spiritually in your relationship. Are you longing for your husband to pray with you and share Bible-reading with you? If he seems reluctant, check out the attitude you communicate to him.

Important issues

Sometimes resentment can arise because important issues have not been discussed before the wedding. Perhaps your church does not run marriage preparation classes, so you have not been made aware of possible causes of tension in your marriage relationship.

You may be committed Christians, filled with the Spirit and longing to serve the Lord together. As a couple you may enjoy times of prayer and Bible study and be ready to share your faith. Your values and spiritual goals in life may be identical, and your desire to know more of God may be mutually strong. But did you discuss whether or not you want children,

when you will have them and how you will discipline them?
Have you discussed money, and whether or not one of you
will stay at home full-time when you have your family? Were
you able to discuss together the effect upon you both of your
husband's (or your own) pre-Christian sexual exploits? How
will you deal with hurts and disagreements – or bigger arguments over big issues? (eg What if he (or you) is offered a job
relocation in another area or another country?) How will you
deal with your partner's need for more space when you would
like to spend every possible moment together? Does he know
about premenstrual syndrome and the effect it can have on
you? (This is a biggie! After about two years of marriage
Richard told me that he was now writing the due date of my
next period in his diary – he said it helped him to be aware of
the possible reason for all sorts of things. . . .)

What about spending money on expensive hobbies, which
were part of life before marriage? Or spending money on
something one of you wants but the other doesn't think is
necessary? And how about your relationship with his parents
and siblings, and his relationship with yours? The differences
in your temperaments and personalities may mean that you
approach both large and small issues in a very dissimilar manner – and if you have never discussed this, there may be fire-
works in your marriage!

Small issues

Sometimes the causes of contention appear to be small: being
late for a meal and failing to telephone (him), spending an
hour on the phone to a friend (you), football – playing or
watching – every Saturday (him), both of you to tea at your
mother's every weekend (you). Men and women are very dif-

ferent (Mars and Venus notwithstanding!) and things which are important to you may be very trivial to him, hardly worth making a fuss about. Honest talking about how you both feel, and a true desire to help one another (regardless of how important or trivial the matter appears to each of you) will make a real difference to your relationship. During the 1970s Paul Simon wrote a song called "You're Kind". The last verse says:

> So goodbye, goodbye
> I'm gonna leave you now
> And here's the reason why
>
> I like to sleep with the window open
> And you keep the window closed
> So goodbye
> Goodbye[1]

Relationships can break down for this kind of trivial reason when there is no open communication or desire to understand and reach a mutual agreement with your partner.

Antidotes to resentment

How do we deal with resentment and its attendant attitudes? If we genuinely desire to be "made new in the attitude of [our mind]" (Ephesians 4:23) we can depend on the help of the Holy Spirit as we set out to do this, and there are several relationship strategies which will help us. We will look at two important areas: understanding and communication.

Understanding

Understanding some characteristics of the male temperament

will help us to have good attitudes in our marriages. It is important to know that men and women differ in their attitudes to problem-solving. For instance, when you and he have had an argument, he will want to make up by having sex. You, on the contrary, are quite determined not to have sex until he apologizes. For him, sex is the equivalent of an apology, and it will take him time to learn that for you, talking the situation through (which will probably include an apology) is necessary before the bedroom scene!

Also, when a woman hits a difficult situation, a husband will often try to help her by giving advice which will sort the situation out. This is not what his wife wants to hear. She does not need to know how to resolve the situation – she'll work out how to do that later. What she needs now is a hug, some warm sympathy and a cup of tea. (The exception to this may be when a primary-school-aged offspring "remembers" at 9 p.m. that he or she has to take a robot/shepherdess/caterpillar costume to school for assembly tomorrow. After the hug-sympathy-tea routine, any woman will appreciate a husband's offer to go to the all-night supermarket for cardboard boxes, silver paint, crepe paper, etc. . . .) A man's way of solving problems (especially his wife's!) is to go for the most direct and often simplistic solution. A woman goes about things differently, and a man has to learn that the most helpful thing he can do at times is to cuddle her and listen to her.

One of the most helpful books I have come across recently is *Hang on . . . I Need To Say Something!* by Gillian Warren (Gazelle Books, now Monarch Books, 1997, £5.99). This down-to-earth book presents helpful insights into marriage for those who are newly married, as well as those who have been married for longer than they care to remember! The quirky illustrations by Jacky Fleming add to the book's impact, and its short chapters and helpful ideas make it a really helpful tool for anyone who is working at understanding her man and improving her marriage.

Communication

Willing and open communication, together with a forgiving heart when mistakes are made (see chapter 1), is a great antidote to resentment and can help us develop right attitudes in our marriage relationships. Keeping silent and suffering after a difference of opinion never solves anything – your partner probably has no idea why you are behaving like this! Men are not good at picking up hints and veiled messages, and it is better to be open about your grievance and how it has made you feel. Discussing the need for open communication at a non-emotive time is a good idea, and working out a strategy for you as a couple to initiate communication when there is a problem. Most men are not good at communication; they see no reason to talk through feelings and problems, and often work on the principle that if something is ignored it will either go away or sort itself out somehow. Either way, the man does not have to do anything about it! He may find it difficult to take you seriously at first, or to understand why certain behaviour causes hurt. His response to your desire for communication may itself cause pain!

I remember on one occasion talking to Richard about my need for him to listen to me when he came in at the end of the day. He would eat his meal while chatting to the children and then disappear to prepare for his evening meeting, committee session or personal counselling engagement. We had one free day a week, on a Monday. We unwound as much as

possible during the day; Richard was often tired after two services on the Sunday, and there were usually ten or twelve people at Sunday dinner (there were six of us to start with!).
Monday evening was usually devoted to the children, as it was
the only evening when Richard had opportunity to be with
them. There was never time for us as a couple to talk together.
One day I tried to explain to Richard that this gave me a problem; I simply could not manage with "occasional" communication. His reply was honest and truthful, but I found it very
painful. "I'm dealing with people's problems all day," he told
me. "I simply do not want to talk about more problems when
I get home. Home is where I need peace and quiet, not you
telling me about your needs. I've had enough of people's
needs by the end of the day."

My reaction to this was fairly predictable! But at least it
highlighted our need to talk about the situation, and we were
able to resolve it as we shared our feelings openly with each
other. We saw that there was a need for us to communicate on
a better level, and made plans to have some "talking time". It
became easier when the younger children started school; we
used to drive out of town on Mondays and walk in the country, talking as we went. We also found it a good plan to sit
down together late on Sunday night and talk about the week
ahead, sharing our plans and commitments and deciding
when we would be able to have time together. We planned
ahead what we would do on our "day off", so that we could
look forward to it. We tried to have an evening out together
as often as we could, which meant arranging babysitters. Even
if we really felt too tired to go out, we enjoyed it once we were
on our way. We realized that it was important for us to have
time and enjoyment together as a couple.

Sexual communication is important too, and for busy Christians it has to be planned for! Scheduling an evening off and an early night is not always easy, but is well worth it in terms of your relationship. You can look forward to it, cook a special meal, get the children into bed early, switch on the answering machine and retreat upstairs with a glass of wine for a candlelit bath and a lazy, romantic bedroom session. Relaxation is the key to this, and a determination not to let *anything* stop you having this time together. Your husband needs to be clear about this and write it in his Filofax as he would any other engagement (possibly using a code word!).

If you do not make special time for your physical relationship, sex can soon become just an occasional event without much significance, usually when you are both tired. You both know it's your Christian duty to have sex in your marriage but somehow the rest of life is so exhausting and time-consuming that there isn't much energy left by your (very late) bedtime. Planning it in advance may sound mechanical but actually works better than just leaving it to happen when you feel like it. Of course, you may feel like it at other times too – and sometimes it happens spontaneously – but planning "the works" on a regular basis deliberately builds romantic love into your marriage and helps your attitudes to remain positive!

Communication between two marriage partners does not mean that you aim to feel and act exactly the same as one another, nor that you will perceive things in the same way. You may be totally different in the way you handle situations, but good communication will mean that you have unity of heart while allowing one another freedom to be different. The strong foundation of your faith in God makes this possible.

Working at communication in a marriage can be a real effort but it is vital. Marriage without good communication can lead to resentment and, ultimately, the kind of boredom which leads to the "separate life" syndrome, where neither of you affirms or encourages the other. And if a person is not affirmed by his or her partner, that person will eventually seek affirmation elsewhere. Sometimes this will lead to an affair, sometimes to total involvement with sport or a hobby and sometimes even to a "fantasy" life. How sad for two people to live through years of marriage with no communication or understanding of one another, and to find their satisfaction in opposite directions!

If you have been abused

Lack of desire for oneness and communication with your partner can be present because of factors in your past, as I said in chapter 1, referring to reactive attitudes. This applies particularly if you have experienced incest or sexual abuse, and it is important that your husband should know what happened to you and that both of you receive help. The book *Child Sexual Abuse – A Hope for Healing* by Maxine Hancock and Karen Burton Mains (Highland Books, 1993) is one you may find very helpful, also *The Wounded Heart* by Dr Dan Allender (published by CWR, reprinted 1993). Perhaps reading a book could be your first step and then you and your husband could go and talk to your pastor, who could help you to find a sympathetic and experienced counsellor. The effects of sexual abuse do not go away by themselves, and you will not be able to have right attitudes to sex or to your own self-image without receiving help.

Communication with God

In chapter 2 I wrote about intimacy with God. Intimacy with God results from communication with him, and good communication with your husband depends on your intimacy and communication with God. This has become very clear to me over the years, as I have observed many marriage relationships and as I have worked at my own marriage. I know that when I am communicating on a regular basis with Jesus and allowing him to fill my mind and heart with his love and his attitudes, only then can I have those attitudes toward my husband. God's grace, mercy and forgiveness extended to me enables me to show grace, mercy and forgiveness to Richard; I can forgive as I have been forgiven. 1 Corinthians 13:5 tells us that love "keeps no record of wrongs" – this is important, and it means I don't present Richard with a reminder of all the previous occasions he has offended me when a new occasion arises!

I also wrote in chapter 2 about being part of God's family, and in the section "Your attitude to the family of God" I mentioned several verses of scripture from the epistles which describe our attitudes to one another. I encourage you to read through these verses and ask God to give you these attitudes toward your husband. If your husband is a Christian, he is the person closest to you in God's family. The more you pray for him like this, the more you will appreciate him. You are the person most aware of your husband's needs, so you can pray for God to meet those needs and to do him good. Your communication with God will definitely bless your marriage relationship!

There may be factors in your marriage relationship which

will change the way you tackle specific issues; for instance, if you are married to a church leader, or married to someone from another culture, or if your husband is not a Christian. Perhaps you are in a childless marriage – and this may be by choice or not by choice. You may even be in an abusive marriage. We will look at some of these situations in the following sections.

Married to a church leader

Marriage to a church leader, vicar or pastor brings its own challenges. Some denominations include preparation for clergy or ministry wives, but most of the "learning" happens on the job! I have a theory, based on much experience, that God uses leaders and their wives (or husbands) as visual aids! If we can deal honestly and openly with our own problems, others will be prepared to share their own problems and needs with us. And as we, through the grace of God, find answers, we will be able to help others who face similar problems. Working through our own problems will give us hope and assurance that those to whom we minister can also come through to a place of hope and peace.

Being in leadership means we must be prepared to deal with our problems – we cannot just leave them and hope things will improve; relationship problems do not usually change for the better by themselves! In the early years of our marriage Richard and I had many "communication problems", largely due to the difficulties and rejection we had experienced in our early family life. At that time we knew nothing about the power of the Holy Spirit to heal wounds in a person's inner being, so for many years we tried unsuccessfully to deal with the difficulties in our relationship. Then, over the years, we began to benefit from the ministry and counsel of other pastors and leaders who helped us. When we received help our church benefited in turn, as we learned to help those in our care.

We recognized that we had to learn to work as a united team, and for me that meant submitting to Richard's headship in marriage as well as supporting his leadership! Our unity was vital as we ministered to others. This was a difficult lesson for me to learn, but one day God underlined it in an unusual way. We had had a rather stormy disagreement; I cannot now remember the cause of it but I know that I was so cross that I was giving Richard the "silent treatment". There was a knock at the front door and when I answered it my friend Joyce, one of the young mums from church, was standing on the doorstep looking embarrassed. "I don't want to hold you up," she said nervously, "but God showed me something this morning and he said I was to come and share it with you."

"Go on," I said.

"Well, when I was praying I saw a picture of a field. Two yoked oxen were pulling a plough up and down the field. Suddenly one of the oxen stood still and refused to move on with the other, so the ploughing had to stop. That's all – sorry if it sounds a bit stupid."

I thanked her and said goodbye, tears in my eyes. God had shown me, supernaturally, what was at stake. Our disunity was a hindrance to the work of God in our patch. I knew my apologies had to come first and that we had to be committed to working through our disagreements. The Irresistible Force and the Immovable Object had, somehow, to become one!

Dave and Joyce Ames, in their book *Marriage in a Hostile*

World, make an interesting comment on the subject of the "headship" of a Christian husband. "Headship does not give husbands the right to assert their will, but the responsibility to exercise sound judgement. The fact is, in a well-ordered family, headship is seldom if ever 'asserted' – it practically goes unnoticed. When a couple enter decisions looking for God's wisdom, they generally find it. 'But the wisdom that comes from heaven is first of all pure; then peace-loving, considerate, submissive, full of mercy and good fruit, impartial and sincere' (James 3:17, NIV). Headship and submission are an integral part of Christian family structure, but marriage is more than family structure, it is two people becoming one. When they are successful at this, headship and submission are obscured by partnership." (*Marriage in a Hostile World*, available from Mission to Marriage.)

When your husband is unpopular

If you are married to a church leader there will be times when your husband is unpopular, when he may make a decision that the church does not find easy to accept. What should your attitude be when this happens?

Some years ago Richard was asked to marry a young couple. The girl was the daughter of a church member, a greatly respected man. She had made a clear profession of faith several years before. But she had drifted away from God, and the young man she wanted to marry made no pretence of being a Christian, though he was a charming young man and loved her dearly. Richard felt he could not conduct the wedding ceremony – he could not be responsible for joining darkness to light (2 Corinthians 6:14), bringing together someone who was a part of the kingdom of God and another who was not.

Many church members supported his decision, which was a hard one for him to make because the girl's parents were our good friends. Others felt he was being too hard on the young couple, who eventually married in another church. I was made very aware that there were two points of view in the church; I knew that I totally supported Richard in his decision, but it was not a good thing to be seen to take sides. The same would have been true had I *not* supported his decision.

You are married to the man, not the job. You may not always agree with decisions he may make with elders or deacons, but you need to have a supportive attitude toward the man, even if you can't toward the plan! Don't become involved in any public or unwise discussion about decisions made by the church leadership. Especially do not become involved in criticizing or undermining your husband or any of his colleagues in leadership; *you* are the only person who will suffer from the rebound effect of this. Talk to your husband or, if you must "let off steam", to a friend who is utterly trustworthy.

Sometimes you will have to deal with the hurt of having your husband's ministry and work rejected. People may leave the church because they do not agree with his preaching or his leadership. These may be people with whom you have shared love and friendship, for whom you have cared spiritually and prayed much. Their leaving will cause pain to your husband and to you, especially if they have not had the courage to come and talk with you about their reasons for going. You will need to have a heart of forgiveness and a willingness to release them and move on from the situation. Going over and over it in your mind will not help you or them. Release them to God, and let him deal with their attitudes – and with yours!

Forgiving your husband after a major disaster

What if your husband makes decisions which ultimately cause pain and hurt for you as a couple? (This does not only apply to those in church leadership.) How can you reach a place of forgiveness? I had to face this in my own life some years ago. Richard had been pastor of our church for many years. It was our life, our work and our source of close friendship and fellowship – in short, our family. Our children had grown up there; two of our daughters had married and were happily settled with their husbands in the church. We had seen the church grow in numbers and in the power and ministry of the Holy Spirit. We had grown out of the church building and it could not be extended, so Richard and the other leaders were praying about our future accommodation. Should we be looking for a bigger building, or starting a "building fund" to erect a new church building ourselves? Should we look for another piece of land, or demolish and rebuild on the present site?

All this was being considered when Richard met another local pastor who had a large church building but a small congregation – the opposite situation to our own. They became friends and eventually decided, after praying about it, to explore the possibility of joining together, using the larger building as church premises and amalgamating the leadership. We began to have joint services, and the two church communities became friends, as did the groups of elders and leaders. It was decided that the two pastors should jointly lead the church. We began to meet together every few weeks for a Sunday service, and for other events. Eventually the time came when we held a service to join our two fellowships together, and from then on we met on Sundays in the larger building. Our two groups of leaders began to work together as a team. But it soon became obvious that Richard and the other pastor were finding it very difficult to work together, and that their pastoral styles were very different. This caused problems both for them and for the newly formed group of leaders.

Richard was often asked to go to other churches to teach or help in pastoral situations, and as the "home" situation became more difficult he found himself accepting more and more invitations for outside ministry. (Afterwards he realized that this had not been a good thing to do; he should have stayed and reassured the church of his commitment to them, as many people became concerned about his continued absence from what was becoming a difficult situation.) The other leading pastor took on more and more of the care of the church, and eventually Richard felt he should resign and move away, so that the other pastor could lead the church in his own way. Their marked difference in leadership styles was making it difficult for the church to remain united. A church in East Anglia had wanted Richard to go and be their pastor for some time, and he decided to accept their invitation.

So we made plans to move to East Anglia. The last few months before we moved were the most difficult I had ever experienced. The other leading pastor did not require Richard to take part in any aspect of the care of the church. Neither of us were able to attend leaders' and wives' meetings, so we lost all our close friendships immediately, as Richard encouraged all the leaders to relate to the other pastor so that there should be no confusion. Richard was still fulfilling engagements at other churches around the south of England, so he was often away. I had been involved in leading the church women's group, as well as groups of leaders' wives, but now I had no involvement with any church activity, so I was very lonely. Most of my close friends had been the other church leaders' wives, and it was difficult for them to visit me, as we were all aware of the painful situation and I did not want to cause loyalty problems for them in their relationship with the new pastor.

Worst of all, our two elder daughters had given birth to beautiful babies within three months of each other, and now we would be leaving them. As a mum, knowing my daughters needed me, my heart was breaking. Our house was put on the market; it sold quickly and we began to pack and prepare for our move. I was finding it impossible to deal with all the loss in my life – loss of close relationships, loss of fulfilling ministry, loss of my home and my loved environment, loss of the near proximity of my two beloved daughters and their new babies. I knew that Richard was dealing with loss too and I wanted to support him, but I had no resources left.

Our move to a coastal town in East Anglia took place on a warm August day. Our youngest daughter and our son came with us, though both of them would be marrying shortly and returning to London. It was good to have them with us for the first difficult months and I was determined to be as helpful to Richard as I could in the new church. Deep in my heart I was angry with him for (as I saw it) bringing about this situation, though he told me it had seemed the only right thing to do at the time. I sought God's help daily, read my Bible and prayed, and began the task of getting to know the people in our new church. They were lovely and welcomed us with open arms. We soon began to make friends, and Richard enjoyed leading the team of elders and house-group leaders.

I began to get used to a routine which involved driving back to London every other week to have time with our two elder daughters and our grandchildren. They came down to stay whenever they could and enjoyed meeting our new friends. I felt that I had dealt with my situation as well as I could but I knew that things were not right. I found it impossible to talk to people on any deep level or to listen to people with serious needs; I just wanted to run away; I was aware that there were desperate needs inside *me* which were not being acknowledged, even by me!

I struggled on for two years, determined to support Richard in his ministry. Our two younger children married and moved away; within a few months of this I began to suffer horrendous headaches every few weeks, which were not touched by the doctor's powerful painkillers and which put me to bed for several days at a time. After a few weeks of this I began to have feelings of utter hopelessness and despair. I dragged myself to the doctor, who diagnosed clinical depression and put me on antidepressants. Our doctor was not a Christian believer, but he was a very understanding person, and asked me a number of questions about my lifestyle and about our family. I had to return to him on a regular basis for the tablets to be monitored, and also because the dreadful headaches were still recurring.

One day I felt so low that I drove down to the sea and parked by the shore on a lonely spot. As I looked out at the grey sea I felt a strong temptation to walk into the waves and just keep on walking; I felt I could not carry on. I knew God was my Father and that he loved me, but life seemed just too difficult. Eventually I started the car and drove away. I knew that I could not hurt my husband and family by taking my life; there had to be another answer. The following week I visited the surgery and the doctor spoke to me very seriously. "I don't know how your husband would feel about this," he said. "But I don't think your health is going to improve unless you move back to London. Your depression is due to factors which won't change, especially the separation from your family."

I told Richard what the doctor had said. He took it very seriously, and we began to pray about the possibility of returning to the London area. When Richard began to share his thoughts with friends who were also in the ministry, many advised him not to move back. They felt that God had brought him to East Anglia and that he should stay there and make that area the focus of his ministry. But Richard felt sure that he should consider my health first; he began to make plans to return to London. He pointed out to me that when we did relocate, he would have to register as unemployed, as there was no church for him to return to and he would have to look for another job. We would have to find a flat, as the national differential in house prices meant that the sale of our house in East Anglia would only pay for a small flat in London. We did not know what we would do about church, as I was by now finding it impossible to sit through a worship service, or talk to people.

After several months, during which time we sold our house and Richard talked with the other leaders about plans for the church, we moved back to London. Because I was on a high dose of antidepressants, I remember very little about the move, only a great sense of relief as we came across the bridge over the Thames on to the A2 major road. We unloaded our furniture into the small flat we had found, and began the next stage of our lives.

As we settled in I began to feel much more normal; we were back living near our daughters, who by now both had second babies, and Amy, my eldest daughter, asked if I would look after baby Alex for three days a week when she went back to work. She insisted on paying me, because as she said, "I'd rather you had the money, Mum, than pay it to a child-minder who won't love him as much as you do!" The money was useful, because it was six months before Richard found another job. Eventually he was appointed as the London representative for an organization which existed to help solvent abusers. He attended training courses on drug abuse, learned how to work and co-operate with the police and local education authorities, and often had to counsel bereaved families as well as helping solvent abusers to kick their habit.

We began to attend the Baptist church opposite our flat, where the services were quiet and predictable; life became more ordered. Under our new doctor I began to lower the dosage of my antidepressants, though it was a long time before I finally had the courage to come off the lowest dose. I had been taking them for more than a year.

As my health became normal, I had to face the fact that Richard had left his calling to the ministry because of me. He was doing his new job very competently; as a pastor he was used to being in contact with the public, and now he was required to take part in radio discussions and make television appearances. Whenever a young person in the London area died from abusing solvents, Richard would be called upon to comment and explain. He liaised with local drug teams, visited schools, went on courses, and told me he had learnt things of which he had been entirely ignorant during all his years of pastoral caring for people. Yet I knew he desperately missed being in the ministry and being free to preach the gospel of Jesus Christ, which is the only real answer for those who are trapped in drug and solvent abuse.

Our relationship was not good; bouts of depression would return for days at a time as I realized the truth of our situation. There seemed no way that Richard could ever return to full-time ministry and, even if he did, I knew I could not support him: I still carried the burden of all the "unfinished business" at the end of our years in London. I did not understand how everything could have gone so wrong and I still felt deeply hurt by the events which had taken us to East Anglia and caused me so much pain while we were there. And now that we were back in London again, none of our previous friends in the ministry had made contact with us. The fact that we were not worshipping in a church which belonged to our own "stream" meant that we were out of touch with churches we had been involved with, and though this was a choice we had made to enable me to attend church without emotional strain, it also meant that we were out of contact with other leaders who had been our friends. I knew this was very painful for Richard, though he made light of it, saying to me that he knew they were all very busy.

One day the pastor of the church we were attending came to see me. He knew our history, and Richard had told him that I was still suffering occasional periods of depression. He spoke to me about seeing a counsellor, as he felt that I needed something more than pastoral care in order to move on from what had happened. He was able to give me the name of a Christian counsellor in Surrey who was experienced in working with pastors' wives, and so I found myself travelling up to Waterloo to catch a train, feeling very apprehensive.

I spent two separate days with the counsellor. She and her colleague gently probed into the rejection of my early life before moving on to look at my relationships, my marriage and the traumatic events of the recent years. My life was stripped bare, and although it was painful it was done with much love and gentleness. I was faced again with the truth of God's sovereignty and of his personal love for me. I was ministered to in the power of the Holy Spirit, and his healing love reached into the hurts inside me. I was also faced with my own responsibility to forgive those who had caused me such pain, and my counsellors asked me to name each person; it was a very long list, and finished with those friends who had ignored us since our return to London. (I am sure it was no coincidence that during the following week we received letters from five of these friends. My releasing forgiveness to them had obviously had repercussions in heavenly places.)

I returned home after the second day of counselling feeling that my life had been unravelled and put back together again. I had been given scriptures which I knew were vitally important for me to read, learn and trust. I had been shown the necessity of forgiving myself as well as others – and I was able to release forgiveness to Richard. Our relationship improved, and we began to pray that God would open the way for Richard to return to the ministry. We couldn't see any way this could happen, so we got on with our present life day by day.

One day some friends came for a meal; they had been our church youth leaders when our children were teenagers, so we knew them well. They had moved house and church a few years before, and invited us to visit their church one Sunday. This was a church from our own "stream", where Richard had been to preach many years before; it was not very far from our old church. The worship was spontaneous and full of praise to God, and we felt at home immediately; we were coming back to our roots! The emotional healing I had received enabled me to participate in free and lively worship once again; we both felt we wanted to join with this fellowship, which proved to be a place of healing and love for us both, though we had been grateful for the care of the church opposite our flat, which had helped us and cared for us through a difficult and painful time. They understood our desire to move back to our own "stream" of church life, though they were sorry to lose us.

We settled down in our new church, appreciating the care of the pastor and leaders, who welcomed us warmly and showed us real and unconditional love. I was still praying for God to open the way for Richard to return to the ministry, and we were amazed and full of praise to God when, a few months later, Richard was asked to join the full-time pastoral team. God had brought us full circle; Richard came back into ministry with a new compassion and care toward those in the grip of drug and solvent abuse, and a new appreciation of the privilege of being in full-time service to the Lord and his people.

We learned much during those years of pain. At one point our marriage could have broken up; we were both full of hurt and unable to comfort each other. But we came through that time with our marriage intact and a greater understanding of each other. We also have a greater understanding of the sovereignty of our God and of how he can cause even our mistakes and our pain to become productive.

Working relationships

Another important factor when you are in leadership is the recognition of "working relationships". You may enjoy wonderful fellowship and friendship with other leadership couples in your church by virtue of your husband's position. Your busy church and family life may not leave time for building up other friendships. Perhaps you attend leadership conferences in your denomination or church "stream" and you feel very secure in your close and committed circle of "leadership friends". But if your own or your husband's leadership responsibility ceases for any reason, you may find yourself bereft of these loving friends who have "come with the job". If they have been your main source of friendship and input you can become very lonely, as can your husband. People do not "drop" you through any malicious intent, it is simply that leaders are very busy people, and if you are no longer part of the circle of leadership there may be no opportunity for contact with you.

When this happened in my own life, as I have described, I made a conscious decision that in future, whether my husband was in a leadership position or not, I would make a point of building good, strong friendships with people who did not have leadership roles. The time came when Richard was once again in a church leadership situation, but I have continued to build "non-leader" friendships which have proved good and rewarding. Once again I have dear friends who are "working relationship" friends, but I know that if our situation should change I would not lose all my friendships at once!

Coping with jealousy

Sometimes a "working relationship" for your husband may mean that he is in a situation which brings him into contact with gorgeous girls; what will your attitudes be if this happens? Perhaps he is involved in training pastoral helpers or cell-group leaders – or he may have a glamorous secretary! As one who has been in this position, I know how important it is to keep your heart free of suspicion and jealousy. Some years ago my husband had a beautiful and efficient secretary, with whom he shared many more hours than he spent with me. I struggled with this, especially as I knew that this lovely girl had a deep commitment to the Lord and was above suspicion; her only desire was to be an excellent administrator and do her work to the glory of God; flirting with Richard would be the last thing on her mind (or on his!). My attitude had to be one of trust towards him and friendship and love towards her. With God's help I came to this position, and to this day she does not know how I felt – though she will if she reads this book and recognizes herself!

If your husband is a church leader, he should understand the importance of making sure he has female support if he is counselling a single woman, and the support of her husband or a woman friend if he is with a married woman; there should always be someone else in the house or the church building where the counselling takes place. This needs to be remembered whether your husband is in full-time leadership or a position of leadership in a house-group or cell-group – or leading a group of Sunday school or Kids' Church leaders. It is not only common sense, but helps you, as his wife, to keep your attitudes right and to trust your husband.

You need support

I realize that I have written a great deal for the wives of leaders, but from many years of experience and of contact with wives of church leaders from several denominations, I believe that they are a group of people who need more support than they get! Men in leadership positions receive a great deal of peer support and teaching; their wives do not. Yet leadership wives need to be able to support and strengthen their husbands, and to do this they need to know they have support themselves; their husbands are not necessarily the people to supply this. Ministry wives need to know that they can have a "listening ear" when they need it, and I believe that church "streams" and denominations should be able to supply counsellors (perhaps on an area basis) who can meet this need.

Married to an unbeliever

In chapter 3, under the section "Dating non-Christians", we looked at some aspects of life in a marriage where one partner is a Christian and the other one is not. As we saw, compromises have to be made, because marriage between a Christian and an unbeliever will clearly produce differences of opinion on many matters such as the use of your time and money, ambition, ethical actions, truth and honesty, the use of your home and the upbringing of your children. The Christian wife's (or husband's) foundation for life will be the word of God; her partner may be committed to a humanistic or otherwise ungodly philosophy or belief, or no belief at all, simply a relaxed assurance that "everything will turn out all right".

I was talking to two friends recently about this, and my

friend Tamsin told me that one of the things she finds hard-
est about being married to a husband who does not walk with
God is the lack of unity in their dealings with their four children. "We often disagree about what the children can watch,
and the things they are allowed to do and the places they are
allowed to go.

"He doesn't mind them watching things that I'm not
happy about, and I do find it difficult. I have to commit this
to the Lord and pray for his protection over the children.
Also, I have to guard my own heart – because I can't help
envying families where both partners are together in Christ
and have the same attitude to their children's viewing and
leisure habits! But I know that God is over my life, and he
knows all about our situation. I have to trust him with Pete
and the children."

Tamsin admits that she finds it hard to be in church on her
own every Sunday while Pete plays golf or tennis. "Our two
younger children, Matt and Miriam, do come to church, but
they sit with their friends so I'm often by myself. I've been
praying for Pete for ten years and I do believe that one day
God's love will reach him and draw him in. God has given me
some promises about that and I'm choosing to be positive and
believe him." Tamsin helps with the children's work at
church, but is careful that her involvement does not cut across
her time with Pete and her family. She told me that in the
early years of her "separate" walk with God she would not
help with any task at church. "I was *so* anxious for God to
work in Pete's life, and when that didn't happen I said to
God, 'You haven't given me what I want, so I'm not going to
do anything for you!' I'm ashamed to admit that now; but
eventually I came to the point where I was able to leave Pete

totally in God's hands, and then I felt free to help with the children's work."

Another friend of mine, Cleo, looks back on 18 years of praying for Chas, her husband. Cleo and Chas have 16-year-old twin sons, Tristan and Toby. Like Tamsin, Cleo believes God is sovereign over her life. She would not have chosen to live in an "unequal yoke", but she recognizes that because of this very fact God has been able to mould her and teach her in a way that has enabled her to help and counsel many others in a similar situation – and also to care with great understanding for the many "single mums" in her church. Over the years she has changed the way she prays for Chas. "I used to beg God to show Chas the error of his ways and his need for God's forgiveness," she said. "But now I ask God to bless him, to do him good. I know that I can't reach him with God's love – only God himself can do that, and I've probably caused Chas problems during the years when I was so desperate for him to see things my way. Now I'm trying to obey God in loving Chas and being his helper, blessing him rather than resenting him."

Both Tamsin and Cleo, together with every Christian woman married to an unbeliever, have to live in two different worlds at the same time. They are part of God's family, needing all the love and security that comes from being in the Christian community, yet at the same time they are part of a family and a community that does not acknowledge God as its head. Sometimes their children will be part of both worlds, too. I have watched many sons and daughters with Christian mums and non-Christian dads who have come with Mum to church until early teenage and then elect to "stay at home with Dad" (especially boys). The exceptions to this are children who have come to a real faith in Jesus and who go to church because they want to be there, not just to accompany Mum. These are the kids who want Dad to come to their baptism service and who pray for his conversion.

If you are in this situation, you need good Christian friends – friends who will not only pray for you, but who will invite you and your family to meals and outings, who will enjoy friendship with your husband without making him feel awkward because he doesn't come to church, and who will happily discuss all kinds of things without turning every conversation into a presentation of the gospel message. (My friend Jane told me about some people she knows who have Bible texts on their walls, their forks, their table napkins and their toilet paper. Apparently they see this as evangelism, but I can imagine that any non-Christian coming into their home would merely think they were two sandwiches short of a picnic!)

Building up good friendships will enable your husband to ask questions about the Christian faith if and when he wants to, and that may not be when *you* want him to. Pray for him, spend quality time together (even if it means you don't get to church every Sunday) and enjoy his company and his love. Don't extend invitations for meals at your home to Christian friends without checking out with your husband that he is happy about it. Invite him to events at church, but don't put him under pressure. Share with him the things you pray for – concerns about the children, pressures in his job, friends with needs – and you may find he appreciates the way you pray. But leave him to God, who knows his heart and how he feels. Have an attitude of trust. The book *Beloved Unbeliever* by Jo Berry (Zondervan, 1981, £7.50) contains material you may find very helpful.

If you are in a church where you are seen as a "single wife", where your husband is not made welcome and other Christians do not befriend him or invite him to their homes and to church events (except to ask him if he'd like to come on the Alpha course), go and see the pastor and ask him to help you find friends who will care about your whole family – not just the wife who helps with the children's work! This is a sad situation, especially if the church is committed to evangelism. A non-Christian husband is not just Alpha-fodder; he is a loved human being for whom Jesus died.

There is a tendency, if you are married to an unbeliever, to think that all your problems would be solved if your partner became a Christian. This is not the case, as I have observed with a number of couples I have known through the years. Obviously there is great rejoicing when a husband comes to faith in Jesus but difficulties usually rise to the surface soon after, and have to be addressed. Misunderstandings arise between husband and wife, and the wife may find her attitudes challenged and be unable to cope with the changes in their situation. Loving pastoral care is needed to help both of them adjust, and friends who can allow both of them to express their feelings and fears.

An abusive marriage

Marital abuse takes many forms, and a woman's attitudes will determine how she reacts to it. The wedding vows we make to remain together "for better, for worse" should not include putting up with abuse, whether verbal, physical, sexual or spiritual. Serious abuse in a Christian home is often hidden – by the wife, who covers up her bruises and forgives her husband every time, believing that by doing this she is doing the will of God; perhaps she even feels that she is suffering "for Christ's sake". There may come a time when she realizes she needs help, but has no idea where to seek it. Her pastor may not be the best person to confide in, unless he has experience in dealing with similar situations, particularly if the husband is a member of the same church. But no woman should stay with a husband who continually abuses her, knowing that she will continually forgive. There are men who can continue to attend church and participate in worship services while abusing their wives or being unfaithful to them – like Brad, whose wife, Rosemary, told of her experiences (chapter 3), or Emily, who suffered severe emotional abuse and rejection (chapter 1).

If a wife is suffering abuse, particularly if there are children, she should first of all try to get her husband to talk about the situation with her and see whether he would be willing to seek help or to receive counselling. He may be unwilling to admit that his behaviour is wrong, therefore no apology or repentance on his part is necessary; conversely, he may be constantly apologizing and promising change – and continuing his abusive behaviour. If he refuses to seek help or counselling and continues with the abuse, he has made it clear that he no longer honours his marriage contract. The wife may not wish to divorce him at this point, especially if she feels strongly that divorce is wrong or if she is a member of a church which teaches that divorce is wrong regardless of the circumstances involved. However, she should certainly make plans for a period of separation, with the option of returning later if her husband is prepared to confess his abuse to the church leadership and to receive help and counselling. She will need help in finding accommodation and may have to take a member of her family or a trusted friend into her confidence. She may feel safer if she plans to leave at a time when her husband is absent from the house.

An older woman may not feel that she has any options if she is in an abusive marriage; she may not have a job or any skills, therefore she is dependent on her husband for money. She may have become used to the abuse because it has gone on for a long time, and her self-image may be so low that she has convinced herself that she deserves it. She may have hidden the abuse for years. I knew a Scottish Christian wife who hid her husband's abuse of herself, and his physical abuse of their two sons, for years; her husband was a minister of the church and forbade her and her sons ever to tell anyone how he was treating them, because it would destroy the church's confidence in him! Incredibly his wife went along with this. A woman in this kind of situation needs help and support in order to free herself from it. An attitude of resignation is not a good attitude to have; she needs to recognize that this way of thinking enables her husband to continue in his sinful behaviour, whether his abuse is verbal, physical or emotional, and that she is actually preventing her husband from taking responsibility for his behaviour.

A Christian wife may feel that acceptance of abusive behaviour shows that she is a "submissive" wife. Two decades ago, "submission" was a buzz-word for many Christian wives who were sincerely seeking to walk with God and to improve their marriages. Christian literature current at the time taught us that our husbands were God's channels of blessing to us, and that obedience to our husbands was on a par with obedience to God. Whatever your husband asked of you, you should obey without question, even if it was not something you would choose to do. God would protect you from any harmful consequences because you were obeying your husband. The example was cited of Sarah in the book of Genesis, who was twice sent by her husband Abraham into situations which put her at risk sexually from pagan rulers (Genesis 12 and 20). In each case God intervened to rescue her from the situation and return her safely to Abraham. (Incidentally, this kind of "submission" was supposed to be an evangelistic tool if you were married to an unbelieving husband; it was implied that your willingness to go anywhere and do anything your husband requested would lead towards his salvation.)

The Bible is as clear on a husband's responsibility to love his wife as it is on the wife's duty to submit to her husband (Ephesians 5:25–33, 1 Peter 3:7). However, this opposite side of the doctrine did not receive the same amount of application, and the imbalance of teaching produced some serious results. There were men who abused their position of "headship" and began to demand from their wives the kind of unquestioning obedience and commitment which took the husbands from a position of "partnership" in their marriages into a position where they became strong authority figures, able to wield power over their wives. If their actions and decisions were questioned, their wives were told that the husbands were fulfilling their God-given destiny and responsibility as "head" over the woman.

During those years I saw many insecure Christian husbands grasp this teaching and use it as an excuse to lord it over their wives and call it "biblical headship". Many began to be more decisive and to be firmer with their children – and this was good if they had been indifferent or lazy previously (or if they had been married to an overbearing and dominant wife and were beginning to stand up to her!). But some men (particularly those who were insecure and whose self-image was low) began to regard themselves as their wife's "boss" rather than her husband, expecting immediate obedience and "putting her down" if her behaviour met with disapproval. I heard men ordering their wives about in a domineering way and undermining them in front of other people – including their children, who were not slow to follow this example of disrespect.

In recent years, teaching on biblical "submission" has become more balanced, and Christian marriage is recognized as a loving partnership of two "equal but different" people. But abuse in Christian marriages still happens. If you are suffering marital abuse and would like to seek confidential advice, you can telephone the Littledale Trust on 01524 770266 or the Association of Christian Counsellors on 0118 966 2207, who will put you in touch with help in your area.

A childless marriage

A marriage that is childless by choice can be extremely happy. Some would question whether it is right for a Christian couple to marry with the intention of remaining childless; surely the "creation ordinance" tells us to "be fruitful and increase in number; fill the earth" (Genesis 1:28)? (We have to decide whether this actually holds good today, in our present vastly overpopulated world – especially as most couples pay fervent attention to limiting their contribution to the earth's fullness!)

Some people decide to delay childbearing until their career is established, which may take several years. Other couples feel no need for a baby; their family is complete as a twosome. Our daughter Katie and our son-in-law Paul spent the first ten years of their marriage childless, fully intending to remain so. They loved travelling and spent most of their holidays exploring other countries. Finance was not a problem, as they were both working, and they enjoyed coming home to their little flat. Both of them are committed Christians; Katie sings in a worship band and they both enjoy being part of a lively church, where they share in the music and teaching and lead the youth group.

"We had a lovely life," remembers Katie. "We loved being together and having no financial problems or responsibilities. We could eat out when we liked, and do exactly what we wanted. We were free and independent – and to be honest, we both felt that a child would have been an intruder into our cosy twosome!"

So what changed? "I had always said to God that if he wanted us to have a baby he would have to change the way I felt," said Katie. "Paul felt the same way as I did about not having children, but we had agreed that if one of us ever changed, we'd both consider it." Three years ago they both left their jobs and set off on a round-the-world trip which took in the USA, Mexico, New Zealand, Australia, Malaysia and Thailand. During that time away, God did dramatically "change the way Katie felt", and Paul too. Richard and I received a telephone call from Byron Bay in Australia, telling us about it. A year later, back in England, they conceived with no difficulties, moved into a new house and told us to look forward to a new grandchild in April! They enjoyed telling their friends about their coming addition and Katie seemed in excellent health.

Thirteen weeks into the pregnancy she went for a nuchal scan, which would determine whether the baby was at risk of being born with Down's syndrome. To their horror and sadness, the scan showed that the baby was dead. The consultant switched off the scanner and talked to them. He told them that the baby had died about five weeks earlier and that Katie would now have to be admitted to hospital urgently for the removal of the foetus and womb contents. Katie and Paul were devastated, and when she came out of hospital a few days later she was grief-stricken and bewildered, questioning God's purposes in her life, which had seemed so clear. She and Paul decided to name their lost baby, and they had a little service together where they gave the baby back to God and said goodbye. They went shopping and bought a beautiful candle-holder to keep as a reminder of their baby.

As the months passed with no sign of another pregnancy, Katie became more and more stressed. "I don't know what to do," she sobbed to me one day. "I feel such a failure. I know that this level of stress works against my getting pregnant, but I'm stressed because I can't get pregnant. That's the only thing that will stop the stress!"

Through those difficult months Katie faced up to many issues in her life, especially the issue of God's sovereignty and her control of her life. Katie had always been an achiever, who would tackle anything and usually succeed. She had made plans for her life which included giving birth to a baby at the time she wanted. She had even planned exactly the kind of clothes the baby would wear and its future career. Now that baby was gone, and Katie had to face the fact that God's plan was different from hers. She found it difficult to see friends who were pregnant or had new babies. Singing in public was very hard for her, as was anything which awoke deep emotion.

"I realize," she said to me one day, "that my maternal instincts, which had been suppressed for the last ten years, all came to life with that pregnancy. I totally bonded with the baby, and now the loss is like an enormous hole inside me."

Many women will identify with Katie's situation – and with her reactions and feelings. Perhaps not so many will identify with her initial desire to remain childless. For the majority of women, having children is a normal expectation; few of us anticipate problems in conceiving and bearing them. When children do not come along as planned, we seek medical help, and often the solution is a simple one or there is treatment or surgery available if the problem proves more difficult.

Sometimes a woman can become pregnant but loses the baby before full term, as Katie did. My friend Mollie had five miscarriages before achieving two full-term pregnancies; in her case the problem was a hormone deficiency but because she and her husband John were serving as missionaries in a remote area of the Middle East at the time, she was not able to receive treatment in time to save any of the babies. When she came home on furlough the problem was diagnosed and she was told to report to hospital immediately she became pregnant again. The hormone injections she received enabled her to maintain the pregnancy and give birth to Nick, and later to Susie. She told me that during the years of her miscarriages she had swung from hope to despair many times, wondering if she would ever carry a baby to full term. After the first miscarriage she and John felt that God had given them a promise from John's gospel: "You will grieve, but your grief will turn to joy" (John 16:20).

"I held on to that word and believed it," she said. "Even when it looked as if I would never have a full-term pregnancy, I trusted God that he would give us what he had promised – joy in the birth of a baby."

Another friend, Annie, wanted children more than anything else, but suffered an ectopic pregnancy soon after she and her husband Steve began trying to have a family. Annie nearly lost her life, and was told afterwards that it was unlikely that she would ever be able to have children. "I was in despair," she said. "I so desperately wanted a family. I shouted at God, feeling that he must hate me, and I told Steve he would be better off with someone else who could give him children. I really didn't see any point in living. It was a terrible time. I felt suicidal, and planned how I could end my life."

Eventually, against all the odds, Annie gave birth to Harriet, who is now nine. "We were so thrilled, and so grateful to God," she remembers. "But then I had two miscarriages, and the disappointment was awful. I found myself saying to God, "Why me again? Haven't I been through enough?" And then, after four-and-a-half years, I had Leo and Oliver. So from thinking I would never have any, I now have three. I'm so grateful to God, especially after the way I shouted at him!"

Grief, depression, anger, feelings of failure and blame are often part of experiencing infertility. You are bereaved of the baby you haven't brought into the world, and deep grief is a part of bereavement. There is depression because you haven't been able to conceive, and anger towards your husband, towards God, even towards yourself because your body doesn't do what it should do naturally. There is often grief for your family, too – for your parents who will never be grandparents, for your brothers and sisters who will never be uncles and aunts.

Mollie and Annie both went on to have babies in spite of their physical problems. And Katie finally became pregnant again; a few months ago she gave birth to Zachary Matthew, a cheerful little chap with whom she and Paul are delighted! But what if no baby arrives after all? What if infertility is permanent? Either partner may have a condition which makes it impossible to conceive. If this is diagnosed, it will end the monthly disappointments which may have continued for years, but it will require both of you to face a situation which you had never expected and which may devastate you.

Mike and Katey Morris's book *Two's Company – Testament of Childlessness* (Kingsway, 1988) describes how they faced the fact of their infertility. For several years they had prayed and longed for a family. After Katey had undergone several gynaecological procedures without success, they considered other options, such as *in vitro* fertilization or adoption, but eventually decided that they would remain as they were – a family of two. At the end of the book Katey writes about her feelings while facing another hospitalization: "This period of treatment was to prove the most distressing and also the last. It also marked that point on our voyage where we discovered that we were whole individuals, in spite of our infertility; that we were complete as a couple, even without children of our own; that God loved us and was everything to us although our constant *cri de coeur* was as yet apparently unheeded." This book is a helpful one for those who are struggling with their attitudes toward infertility. Another useful book is *Some Mothers Do Have 'Em – Others Don't – A Christian Approach to Infertility and Childlessness* by Hugo and Sharon Anson

(Eagle, 1997), which gives helpful medical information as well as testimony.

I have not experienced childlessness, so I cannot write from personal experience. But I have felt the pain of friends who live with this as they struggle to come to terms with their situation and to recognize and embrace God's plan for their life, which seems so different from what they expected. Moving on from attitudes of bitterness and resentment is not easy, but only as we do move on can we experience God's peace and allow him to take us on to the next stage of our life.

There are other marriage situations at which we could look if space allowed; marriage to a partner from another country or culture, or marriage when one partner is disabled or has a chronic illness. Every marriage is as different and individual as the partners belonging to it. But we have seen how positive Christian attitudes can make a difference to actions and reactions in a marriage, and can help us to move forward from negative or stalemate situations into realistic change and hope.

To consider: Did you come into marriage with any unreal expectations? If so, can you see what caused them?

If you can see your own experience reflected anywhere in this chapter, can you think of one positive action you can take which would improve your situation?

Note

1. *You're Kind* by Paul Simon, 1975, from *My Little Town*, by Columbia Music, USA.

CHAPTER FIVE

SEASONS OF MOTHERING

Pregnancy and birth have a fascination for all women who are pregnant and have given birth; "old" and "new" mums are at one in this, whatever their age. I gave birth to my first baby eleven months after our wedding. We hadn't planned for this to happen and thought we had made sure it wouldn't! But when we saw our beautiful baby daughter we thanked God for her and acknowledged his sovereignty.

From the moment our babies are born, our desire as mothers is to protect them and keep them from harm. Even the immunizations they receive at the baby clinic are painful for us to watch, and if you are a first-time mum the sight of the needle pushing into your baby's flesh can have a real shock-horror effect, in spite of the fact that you know these vaccinations are important for your baby's health. As your baby grows through toddlerhood you suffer with him or her through every sickness and pain, every childhood infectious disease. Your love and concern for your baby is absolute, an emotion so powerful that you may be surprised by the strength of it.

The birth of a baby demonstrates to us powerfully how

God feels about us, his children. His heart toward you is as tender as your own love for your baby, and he watches over you with an even greater degree of love and concern. To me it was an awesome thing to realize, as I watched each of my gorgeous babies feed and grow, that my heavenly Father felt the same full-hearted love and commitment towards me as I felt for my children. He rejoiced in my growing understanding of his love and his ways, just as I rejoiced in my babies' growth and increase in understanding. The first smiles, the first conscious grasp of a toy, the first baby-held spoonful of food reaching the mouth (rather than the hair!) – all of these were stages which called forth rejoicing and praise from proud parents.

Our children shape us

Lizzie, a childless friend of mine in her 40s who is a wonderful artist, once said to me that she had never planned to have children. "Once you have kids, you become a hostage to fortune," she said firmly. Lizzie is not a Christian, and the prospect of coping with the risks and stresses of a family was not something she was prepared to contemplate. I have often thought about Lizzie's comment and her motives for remaining childless. Because we are Christians, we have the help and strength of God as we parent our children; we have the truth of the Scriptures to depend on and we have the love and fellowship of the family of God to support us. No way are we "hostages to fortune"!

God will use our children, by their very existence, to shape and mould our lives. How else could we learn to manage on such a small amount of sleep? When I fed my babies at night

I felt as if I were the only person awake in the whole of London. I used to be a shy person, too; having children brought me "out of my shell". It's difficult to hide away when your son is Joseph in the playgroup nativity play, or when you are reading the story of Peter Rabbit (doing all the voices) to a feverish toddler in the surgery waiting-room and look up to see a crowd of enthralled patients hanging on every word.

Our children reflect our attitudes

From the moment our children are born we are deeply involved with them: loving them, protecting them, communicating with them, teaching them and enjoying them. The way we do this will affect our child's growth and development, determining the kind of adult into which he or she will grow. We do not always realize how much our children reflect and reproduce our attitudes and reactions. Consciously or unconsciously, we communicate to our children attitudes of materialism or contentment, cynicism or faith, selfishness or generosity. We communicate *what we are*, regardless of what we say.

Some years ago we knew a couple with a large family of five children. This couple, though Christians, always had problems in their relationships with other people; they took offence very easily, and when their church leaders tried to help them they saw it as "interference in their lives". Any kind of adverse circumstance was always someone else's fault. It was invariably the other child who had deliberately tripped up little Darren or run his bicycle into little Tracy. The teacher was very unfair to be so hard on Martin just because he hadn't done his homework. A few years later poor Ruthie's employer was so unreasonably angry with her for being late every morning that week; the harsh policeman didn't seem to understand that John hadn't *meant* to ride his motor bike through the red light . . . Because these parents would never acknowledge their children's bad behaviour or their need for correction, the children grew up with exactly the same attitude, finding it impossible to admit to any wrongdoings or failures; therefore they were never able to receive help or instruction. It is easy to see what will be reproduced yet again when they have their own children.

Children believe implicitly what we tell them. Our two younger ones went through a phase of not liking school; I thought they were too young for a lecture on government and politics, so I simply told them that the Queen had made a rule that children over five had to go to school every day. They believed me, and the school fuss stopped. One day I heard Katie say to Andy, "When the Queen's dead we can stay at home all the time." (Happily, the Queen remained in good health.)

We make our own decisions about what we tell them regarding Father Christmas and the Tooth Fairy, and they will believe us because they trust us. If they hear us in detrimental discussion of the vicar's or pastor's Sunday sermon, or gossiping about other members of the church, they will believe that, too. If we are critical of somebody privately in the home, but friendly and committed to him in public, our children will also grow up to be less than honest in their relationships. We may really want our children to learn to live righteously, but if we display hypocritical attitudes they will be reproduced in our children.

Our children need boundaries

Yes, this is about discipline – but I think "boundaries" is a better word, and it includes discipline. Boundaries, or behaviour limitations, need to be learned by our children if they are to enjoy relationships in the family, the playgroup or nursery, school, kids' clubs, sports clubs, college or university and, eventually, their workplace.

Boundaries are the way we train our children and set limits on their behaviour. As Christians we have foundational principles, and we will want to teach and interpret these to our children. A few definite rules of behaviour will be necessary. If you don't set these boundaries, your children will not learn self-control, which plays an important part in their self-image and self-esteem. Also, known boundaries give children a foundation for making decisions and choices, and this is one of the things which helps them to learn independence. Setting limits on behaviour will help a child to establish awareness of control over what he or she does (or doesn't do). We should not be afraid to set boundaries for our children.

In 1 Kings 1 and 2 we read the sad story of Adonijah, the selfish son of King David, who attempted to steal the throne of Israel from Solomon, David's rightful heir. Chapter 1, verse 6 says of Adonijah: "His father had never interfered with him by asking, 'Why do you behave as you do?' He was also very handsome . . ." Our children need to be taught boundaries early; this is not always easy, especially if they are "handsome" – saying "No" to a delightful and endearing two-year-old is something we do not enjoy! But our word must be reliable if we are to have credibility with our children; if we have said that pulling the cat's tail again means no *Teletubbies*, and we hear the cat's yowl a few minutes later, the television must remain firmly off, even if the two-year-old out-yowls the cat!

Setting boundaries, requiring obedience and enforcing loving discipline and correction builds character in our children. Conversely, lack of discipline on our part indicates lack of concern for their character. Some parents are fearful of disciplining their children or setting boundaries on their behaviour; they don't want their children to dislike them, or they can't face the confrontation which ensues when correction is necessary.

Consistent discipline is hard work, but the results are worth the effort. If a child refuses to stay in his bed and continually appears downstairs after the story, the drink of water and the goodnight prayer, it is tempting to allow him to stay with you and play with his toys until he falls asleep on the sofa an hour or two later. Taking him firmly back to bed time after time requires commitment and determination, but unless you are prepared to allow him to deliberately disobey you on a regular basis (to say nothing of having him around all the evening when you and your husband want some private time) this is what you will need to do – even if you cancel every other evening engagement for a fortnight, while you establish the bedtime routine.

The above situation is just one example, but you can be sure that if your child sees that your word can be disobeyed with impunity over the matter of bedtime, it can be disregarded in any other situation he doesn't like. If you eventually "give in" and allow him to stay downstairs, you will eventually "give in" over his wanting sweets before lunch, his not eating lunch because he's had sweets, his screaming because he doesn't want to be left with a babysitter (even if it's

Grandma or someone equally familiar) while you and your husband have a longed-for evening out, his refusal to share any toys with a visiting friend, etc. If all his demands are eventually met and there is no correction or discipline, a child will assume that the world revolves around him – yet at the same time he will feel insecure, because small children are not able to handle this kind of power. They need boundaries, and if they do not have them they will push more and more for their own way, seeing how far they can go. We, as parents, need to give them the security of limits, so that they are aware that disobedience will have consequences.

Boundaries are for mums as well as for children. If our children are continually disobedient and unco-operative, we will eventually find ourselves with an attitude of resentment towards them for the time we have to spend getting them to do things which in themselves take very little time. Setting boundaries for our children will help our own attitudes to be positive and affirming. Later in the chapter we will look at how we can develop attitudes which will help us to build up our relationships with our children.

What about punishment?

The debate on smacking as a form of punishment continues unabated. Today, the "politically correct" view presents smacking as "violence against children". Those who oppose smacking children often refer to it as "hitting" or "cruelty". Yet the Bible tells us clearly: "He who spares the rod hates his son, but he who loves him is careful to discipline him" (Proverbs 13:24). Later in the book of Proverbs we read, "Folly is bound up in the heart of a child, but the rod of discipline will drive it far from him" (Proverbs 22:15). Physical correction by loving Christian parents (whether it is carried out with the hand or the ubiquitous wooden spoon) is not violence or cruelty (though it could become so, as could any punishment meted out in a harsh, uncontrolled, heat-of-the-moment reaction to a child's behaviour). It is not a cold-blooded or cruel action, as some would present it. It is a controlled and loving discipline, used in order to teach respect for rules, authority and other people. Children need to know that certain actions will have consequences; they learn this quickly, and physical discipline, if used correctly, will not be needed for long.

Those who oppose smacking often feel that verbal argument and reasoning with a child is preferable. Fine, if you have the sort of child who will respond positively – most, in my experience, do not! Verbal argument often degenerates into something worse. I have personal experience of this; my mother did not believe in smacking or punishing children in any way. Her tongue was her only weapon, and she made good use of it. If I was naughty she called me names, and the more I misbehaved the worse her verbal onslaught became. The horrible names she called me went very deep; I could never talk about their effect upon me until many years later, when a Christian counsellor questioned me about my childhood and my mother. She asked me to tell her the names my mother had called me; it was a struggle to voice those words which had hurt me so much, and it was a long time before I could get them out. The counsellor pointed out to me that words and name-calling can wound a vulnerable child deeply, and as she talked to me I realized that many of the words and names my mother used had caused the tremendous sense of rejection that had been a powerful factor in my life and my relationships. She showed me that Satan can use these names as weapons against Christians, telling us that they are true descriptions of us.

The counsellor and her colleague began to pray for my freedom from the effect of the verbal abuse. My mother would frequently shout at me, "You vile creature!" As the counsellor prayed for me, she turned this phrase against Satan, who is the original "vile creature"; the awful power of this description was lifted off me at last. Many other words and names were dealt with that day, and I am so grateful for the power of the Holy Spirit who can bring healing to deep hurts from our past. How much better it would have been if my mother could have administered a corrective smack rather than words which caused so much long-term pain! I determined that I would *never* call my children names or verbally abuse them in any way. We used the biblical method of physical correction, and all our children have told us that they knew this was done with love and that it was for their good.

(NB I would like to add here that my mother died several years ago, and that my father died last year; only because of that do I feel free to write about the experiences I have just shared. When my children reached adulthood I told them what my early childhood had been like; my daughters pointed out to me that I had already broken the link of verbal abuse which so often affects several generations of a family, because I had never shouted at them or called them names.)

As they grow older

As children grow, and certainly before they reach their teens, other forms of correction and punishment are needed, and this will vary according to what is suitable for a particular child. For a child who enjoys reading, being "grounded" in his room will not be a memorable punishment! For some children, being "grounded" at home for a few days may make your point, or losing pocket money, or being banned from using the internet or watching television. It's a good idea to have a clear understanding from the beginning about what is the "punishment policy" in your family; then everyone knows where they stand.

Self-discipline

Our children need to see why discipline is necessary in their lives, and they also need to see that we have discipline and boundaries in our own lives, that we cannot do or have everything we want, that choices have to be made about how we live and how we use our time and our money; this will apply to many different areas, from regular Bible-reading to household chores and honesty in the workplace! The more we learn self-discipline, the easier it will be to teach it to our children. We can talk to them about how God disciplines us and how we respond to him. As we saw in chapter 2, discipline is a response to God's grace, not a legalistic pattern of life. We can share with them the reasons for God's discipline in our lives – Hebrews 12:10 tells us that "God disciplines us for our good, that we may share in his holiness."

Protecting our children

We saw earlier that the desire to protect our children from harm comes with the first baby. We are made aware of the danger of cot-death, so we put our babies down in the "safe" position. We put a net over the pram outside to keep insects away. We test the bath-water. Once they are toddlers, protection becomes big business. We have stair gates, cooker guards and socket plugs; we remove dangerous objects; we put child-proof locks on cupboards. But the time comes eventually when a toddler has to be taught how to manage the stairs, and why fires and irons are dangerous to touch. Sometimes, in spite of our watchfulness, they learn the hard way. One of our small daughters was very curious about our gas cooker, which had a pilot light with a small metal cover over it. This was very hot, as the pilot light was always burning, and the children were forbidden to touch it. One day four-year-old Leigh pulled a chair up to the cooker, climbed on to it and put her finger on the interesting metal cover. The resulting sizzle and shriek meant that we never again had to warn the children to keep away from the cooker!

As children grow we continue to protect them, warning them and teaching them about traffic danger, care when using buses and trains, not talking to strangers and being sensible about where they go. The time comes when we also warn them about drugs, solvents and paedophiles. The more they learn, the safer they will be. And as Christian parents, we want them to know Jesus and to be built up in their faith so that they will be able to protect themselves morally and spiritually in a world which has walked away from truth and righteousness.

Teaching our children a foundation for life

When our children start playgroup and school we have to begin trusting others to protect them; but we need to continue to teach them the truth of God, which will be a foundation for their lives. This will be their greatest protection as they grow up in a world where they will learn from school, from their friends, from television programmes and from the internet all kinds of things which will be presented as truth. They will be told that sex in your teens is fine as long as you act responsibly, that the occult is interesting to explore, that gay and lesbian partnerships are as valid as heterosexual marriages, that money, possessions and clothes are the sum of a person's identity and that if something feels good and doesn't hurt anyone else, go for it!

Biblical truth, which your child is learning at home, will clearly differ from many of these things learnt at school and from other sources. We need to ask God for right attitudes, wisdom and the power of the Holy Spirit if there is a conflict between home and school – especially if Teacher is flavour of the month! It is helpful to build a good relationship with your child's teacher, so that if a situation arises where you have to disagree with him or her, you are already on friendly terms.

When our children are tiny, and even before they are born, we pray for them and lift them to God. As they grow, this constant affirmation of God's presence will help them to recognize him as a reality in your life and in their lives, too. We can teach them Bible stories and show them how God's word speaks into our situations and problems. We can pray with them about friends at playgroup and at school, and about their needs and ours as a family. We can talk to them about Jesus and his love for them. When they are sick we can lay hands on them and pray for him to heal them and comfort them. As they grow in their awareness and understanding of his love and power, their faith will grow, too – and may even outstrip our own.

I will never forget the occasion when six-year-old Katie

asked Jesus to heal her hands. She had clusters of disfiguring warts all over both of them and none of the doctor's lotions and paints had had any effect. The warts were always catching on her clothes and were a thorough nuisance, although they were not causing her any pain. One evening when I was putting her to bed, we talked about a Bible story she had been reading, about Jesus healing a sick person. "Do you think Jesus would heal my hands?" she asked. "I'd like to pray and ask him to." Her faith had been stirred by what she had read. I wasn't feeling the same faith as Katie but how could I say "No"? We sat on the bed, closed our eyes and very simply asked Jesus to take away the horrible warts from her hands. When we opened our eyes the warts were still very much there. "Let's wait and see," I said, seeing her disappointed face. "I'm sure Jesus heard your prayer." I was sorry about her disappointment, and sad that no healing had apparently taken place. But over the next few days Katie's warts began to disintegrate and, as they crumbled away, clear skin appeared on both her hands. After a week there was no indication that she had ever had a single wart. She was delighted, and we couldn't keep our eyes off her lovely smooth hands. Jesus had honoured her faith, not mine – on that occasion I hadn't had any!

Hebrews 5:14 tells us that "solid food [God's word of truth] is for the mature, who by constant use have trained themselves to distinguish good from evil." That is what we want for our children – that they may be able to discern good from evil, in a world where the two are frequently confused. As we saw in chapter 2, this ability only comes from learning the truth of God's word and taking it into our hearts as a foundation to which everything else relates.

Deuteronomy 6:6–7 tells us to *impress* God's truth upon

194 A GOD FOR ALL SEASONS

our children; this means living our own lives according to God's truth. We cannot teach our children truth if our own attitudes are ambivalent. Children will quickly see through a commitment which is half-hearted. To educate your children in truth you must nurture your own spiritual life. It could be helpful for you to read chapter 2 of this book again, asking God to highlight any areas in your life where there is any need for a change in your attitude toward God, your family or your church.

Our attitudes to mothering

You have looked forward with tremendous anticipation to the birth of your first baby, enjoyed all the preparations and the buying of tiny clothes and baby equipment, learned all you can at the antenatal classes, read all the recommended books, checked out the right websites and, at last, produced the world's Number One Baby. All the excitement is over, your tired husband has returned to work and you are now in charge of this noisy, messy, wonderful little human being. Life has changed out of all recognition.

Attitudes of false pride ("I'm sure I can cope, thanks") or reluctance to accept help should have no place in your life at this point. If you have a demanding baby and are getting very little sleep it's important to take advantage of every offer of help. (I was amused at a recent church coffee morning to hear my friend Sara say to Tracey, another friend who was about to give birth, "I can't do much to help you practically, but if you need to scream or shout or cry, I'll be at the other end of the phone." I never did hear whether Tracey availed herself of this!) When family members or friends are happy to cook a meal or take a pile of ironing, accept gratefully. If you already have a toddler or other children, let willing friends look after them or collect them from playgroup or school. There will be days when getting yourself and the baby dressed and producing an evening meal will be the sum total of your achievement – and sometimes the evening meal will have to be a take-away. As much as you can, sleep or rest when the baby sleeps. After my daughter Leigh had her second baby she said to me that she could understand why people took drugs. "I've got that sort of feeling about sleep, now that I'm getting so little of it," she said. "It's a real craving. If sleep were available as a drug, I'd kill for it!"

Eventually life settles down, Baby sleeps through the night and a routine establishes itself. And after a while, in spite of your loved and longed-for baby, you may find yourself feeling strangely bored and frustrated. Perhaps your thoughts keep returning to the job you left. You love your baby to bits, but his company doesn't give you much mental stimulus. If you already have a toddler and are geared to Teletubbies, Tweenies and Bob the Builder, you may feel overwhelmed by the trappings of nursery life and think your brain is shrinking, especially if the highlight of your week is the mums' and toddlers' group. For an intelligent Christian woman who has had a challenging and interesting job, as well as being involved in service and ministry at church, life at home with a small baby and/or toddler, may prove very boring. If this is you, how can you deal with it and improve things?

Recognizing the season

An attitude which accepts that this is God's present "season" for your life will help you to adjust to the needs of the moment, rather than feeling resentment for the limitations on your lifestyle. Plan a strategy which will fit in with the baby's needs and will also fulfil some of your own. For instance, if you are a keen reader who now has very little time to read, keep a pile of books by the chair where you usually feed your baby. I know we're supposed to spend feeding times bonding, but a book propped up near at hand won't stop that. It's good to listen to music when feeding, too. If you already have a toddler, keep some toys which are only played with while you are feeding the baby, and are put away afterwards. (This helps to counteract the competition for your attention which often happens at feeding time.)

You may not be able to organize a regular Bible-reading and prayer time for months, but you can still take in the word of God and feed yourself spiritually. A Bible verse stuck on your washing-machine, on your bedroom mirror, even on the handle of the baby's buggy to meditate on as you walk, can help you to receive from the Lord and to focus on him. You can change the verse each week, and a good one to start with is Philippians 4:6. You may want to keep this one going for several weeks; "peace" may be something in fairly short supply at this particular time!

The "season" of babies, toddlers and young children will last for a long time, and it is important for you to make the adjustments which will help you live positively. If you are continually saying, "When he sleeps through the night . . .", "When she's out of nappies . . .", When he starts playgroup . . .", "When she's at school . . .", you will always be looking at the future rather than enjoying the present.

I remember my friend Wendy saying to me when her children were small, "I know that this is a season in my life for learning wisdom from God and storing it away. Later on, when the children are older, will be the time to bring out what I've learned and use it to help people. For now, I need to concentrate on the children." Wendy's children have all grown up now, and she has a wide and happy speaking ministry to conferences of women in this country and abroad, as well as being the author of several books. She recognized the "season" of her life and made a conscious decision to be content in it; God honoured her choice by enabling her, many years and experiences later, to share her wisdom helpfully with other women. In our own church we have used Wendy's book *Mainly For Mothers* as the basis for some excellent "parenting" sessions (*Mainly For Mothers* by Wendy Virgo, Kingsway, 1997, £5.99).

See this season of life as God's time for you to learn from him and demonstrate his love to your children as you take time to teach them the things they need to know – and most of all, about Jesus and what he means to you.

If you are a working mum, you may feel that some of this chapter is irrelevant to you, because you are not the one who makes many of the weekday choices for your child. You may be working part-time or even full-time. If you do work, aim to find a Christian child-minder who will have your values and vision for your child. Someone who shares your faith and who will look after your child using the same principles will mean that your child does not become confused by differing methods of discipline and lifestyle. My own experience of several years as a child-minder for Christian families made me realize that consistent childcare methods bring security into a child's life when he has to be looked after by someone other than his own mum or dad. It may not always be possible for you to find a Christian child-minder, but do find one who will be happy to follow your instructions regarding the care of your children.

Demonstrating love

Earlier in the chapter we looked at how we teach truth to our children, and we need to recognize that our own attitudes toward them will help or hinder them in receiving the truth we are teaching. Just as our loving Father looks on us with love, compassion and affirmation, so we need to have these same attitudes toward our children. This is not always easy, but it helps if we recognize that our children often inherit character traits from us which the grace of God has dealt with and enabled us to control in our own lives. This gives us hope and encouragement to pray for our children. What God has done in us, he can do in them. You may find that your most difficult child is the one who is just like you used to be! This will help you to understand that child's needs and aspirations, and to help your son or daughter to grow and develop his or her character and individuality.

Our children need unconditional love and approval, and physical affection with lots of cuddles and hugs. Dads, too, need to affirm their children (both boys and girls) in this way, regardless of today's suspicious climate. Children also need forgiveness for their misbehaviour (so much easier to impart when proper discipline is in place) and a loving manner of communication from us.

Demonstrating love can take different forms at different ages. Some years ago a national newspaper ran a series of cartoons. "Love is . . ." was captioned on to various pictures showing different loving scenarios. At the time, I put together a few of my own:

Love is . . . spending time in the supermarket greengrocery section searching for apples of a certain greenish-yellow colour which are the only ones a certain daughter will eat . . .

Love is . . . learning all the names, ages and favourite breakfast cereals of the entire Liverpool football team, in order to discuss them with my son . . .

Love is . . . getting up at the crack of dawn every Saturday to take them to Duckling Club at the local swimming baths (I have to be honest, this was Richard, not me – but it certainly demonstrated his love, not just to them but to me, enjoying a cup of tea and a child-free lie-in!).

Love is . . . staying up *very* late with a teenager who needs to talk . . .

Love is . . . making a huge wedding cake of chocolate sponge covered with chocolate icing and Smarties . . . which didn't do much for our image, but was exactly what the bride, our youngest daughter, wanted.

No doubt you can make up a few of your own, and it's a good exercise to see some of the ways in which your love is being demonstrated to your children.

Helping your children to see themselves positively

Affirming and loving our children unconditionally will help them to see themselves positively; this is vitally important for children. It is never a good idea to compare siblings; every child is different, with different abilities and rates of development, and we need to rejoice in the individuality of each one of our children. Some children are born with special needs and will take a long time to reach their potential. Children in this situation need continual encouragement, and their parents need a good support system.

My friend Rene has a son with severe learning difficulties. Richard is now a young adult, sharing a supervised house with several other similarly disabled young men. When Richard was a small child, Rene determined that in spite of his disability, he would learn as much as possible. He attended a special school, but before he started there she taught him to dress himself and to sit at the table and eat a meal properly. (These things are often difficult for children like Richard.) He loved music, so she sang to him all the time and taught him songs. She often came with him to stay with us, and he loved playing with our children. One day Rene said to me, "You know, I love Richard just as he is; I don't want him any other way. I don't pray for his healing, because that would make him a different person. I know his future is in God's hands." There were times when Richard's behavioural problems worried and frustrated her, but because her own attitude was very positive she was able to teach him in a way that helped him, even with his limited ability, to regard himself positively and to learn a great deal more than would have seemed possible.

I am sure this will also be true for James, who was born last year to my friend Cath's daughter, Helen. James has Down's syndrome, so is likely to be late learning how to do some things. But Helen, who is a nursery teacher, is determined that James will have every opportunity to learn everything possible! He is a very sociable baby and enjoys the company of his many young cousins, as well as all his friends at church who pray for him and give him love and affection. James will certainly grow up to see himself positively.

A child with a long-term illness can be a difficult challenge. Julie Sheldon's remarkable book *One Step at a Time* (Hodder & Stoughton, 2000, £5.99) describes with honesty and candour the illness of her ten-year-old daughter Georgie, who was diagnosed with a malignant brain tumour four years ago. Through the years of pain and medical treatment Julie has developed attitudes of endurance and perseverance, and she is still caring for her daughter, whose recovery is slow. Julie shows in the book the importance of helping a child see herself positively in a very negative situation, and I would recommend this book to anyone in a similar position who needs encouragement and understanding.

Loving yourself – attitudes and practicalities

As a mum, whether married or single, you need a good support network. But you also need to have an attitude of love toward yourself. There is a great deal of literature available about loving your husband and your children, but unless you are able to love yourself you will not be able to love them to the best of your ability. Loving yourself means looking to your own needs and seeing how these can be met. If your needs always come last, you will eventually collapse physically and emotionally or else begin seriously to resent the demands your family makes upon you.

Josh McDowell and Norm Geisler have written an excellent book called *Love is Always Right*, subtitled *The Key to Making Right Moral Decisions in an Age of Relative Values* (Alpha, 1997). This readable and helpful book includes a chapter called "Loving the Person in the Mirror", where they give three reasons for loving ourselves: first, because we are made in God's image (Genesis 1:26); second, because Jesus commanded us to love others as we love ourselves, showing that self-love is the basis for loving others; and third, because God loves us (1 John 4:10) and if we do not love ourselves, then we are not loving what God loves – and, as the authors point out, it's never a good idea to oppose God!

Being in control

Being in control of your life will help you to love yourself and have a positive attitude. When our children are small we often feel that life controls us rather than the other way round, so it is important that we look at ways of bringing order and control into the way we live our lives and look after our families.

We saw in chapter 2 the importance of feeding ourselves spiritually, and earlier in this chapter we looked at a few more ways of doing that when children are very small. It is probably in the areas of time and energy that we will find our greatest battles, and it is a good idea to look at your situation and think of some practical ways to love yourself by achieving a bit more of both! You may be receiving help from family and friends, but there are practical ways to help yourself and have positive attitudes when the pressure is on. I remember my own list of "sanity-savers" – perhaps some of them can help *you*!

Anticipate! Do as much as you can in advance. (Have the argument with your three-year-old about what she will wear tomorrow on the previous evening, then you can put out her clothes before she goes to bed.)

Rotate batches of toys every three months; the "new" lot will be welcomed as if they really were.

Give everyone in the house a specific job which they do on a regular basis. (Even a 2½-year-old can carry his empty plate to the sink or dishwasher.)

In the school holidays, make a "job box". Mine was an old

shoebox with about 20 postcards in it, each one with a job written on it. When I started this, the jobs were for three- to five-year-olds and nine- to ten-year olds (the ages of my children at the time). During the holidays each child picked a card, turned it over to see which job they had to do and returned the card to the box when they had completed it. Small Katie liked this arrangement because it put her on a level with the three older children – even if she had to have her card read to her! (Pictures can be used for younger children, eg a brush and dustpan, or a box with toys in it if the job is to tidy away toys.)

Collect together a list of possible outings and interesting things to do for the holidays, so you have the information to hand when you want to make plans. (The "cards-in-a-box" system could be useful here, too, and could save the usual arguments about the Natural History Museum versus the local adventure playground; we do whatever comes out of the box!) There is an excellent website, www.planit4kids.co.uk, which you and your children can surf in advance to find out events and amenities in different areas of the country.

During the holidays, plan to have lunch each week with a friend who has children; also plan to invite a friend with children for lunch once a week. Have a friend's children once a week and let her have yours once a week; this will give you both a few child-free hours.

(It looks from this as if I planned the holidays like a military operation – but let me assure you that we did have relaxed, "do-nothing" days, too!)

Have plenty of books available from the moment your children are born; encourage them to read widely and to enjoy visiting your local library (which will probably have "story hours" and craft mornings during the school holidays).

Keep your internet-linked computer in the family living-room, not in your child's bedroom; you will be able to monitor what he or she sees. Find some good websites for helping with homework and keeping your own knowledge up to date. (An excellent one is www.37.com, which will immediately put you in touch with the best of 37 search engines for the subject you want to investigate.)

Teach your children to share; use a kitchen timer to allocate turns on the swing or the computer. This can also be used for exam revision – one hour's work followed by 20 minutes' break.

As soon as children are old enough, teach them to make sandwiches and prepare simple food.

Call a "family conference" if things are tense; this gives everyone a voice in a non-emotive atmosphere. I still have the "minutes" (taken by the eldest child) of one we held years ago. One of the hotly discussed matters was the failure of several family members to replace the loo roll with a new one when they used the last of the current one. A motion was passed (sorry!) committing each "last user" to putting out a new loo roll. The minutes of this meeting also note an increase in pocket money for the younger members of the family.

All these ideas relate to your children and your family life, and will help your children learn to be organized. But there are other things you can do which will help you personally. Take note of the "time of the month", and be gentle and forgiving with yourself (and others) just before your period. Make sure you and your husband have a united front regarding discipline, and don't allow your children to play you off

against each other. Have a definite "personal space" somewhere in your day without feeling guilty. You need it, and
both you and your family will benefit if you have it. You may
feel tempted to get on with "child-free" tasks when you have
some time alone, but use some of that time for *you*.

Remember what you were like before God saved you and
began to work in your life to change you? As we saw earlier,
we should not be surprised to see character traits in our children which were once in us to a greater degree than now.
Recognizing this will help you to have a gentler attitude
towards your children and to pray for them with understanding. Their battles and struggles have been yours, too.

Remember that the phases of childhood and teenage *are*
phases – they don't last for ever. Problems will be worked
through eventually; we will make mistakes, but God and our
children will forgive us, and damage can be repaired. Our
eldest daughter once said to us, "When you have love and
security and acceptance at home, you forget the mistakes."

Attitudes during the teen years

Your teenagers inhabit a very different world from the one in
which you lived as a teenager. "Teenage" attitudes seem to
begin earlier and earlier; your nine-year-old son has to have
the "right" hair gel; your daughter is twelve going on twenty.
We may be apprehensive as they approach their teen years,
wondering if they will drift away from God and from us.
There are things we can do to keep our attitudes positive, and
one of these is to educate ourselves about the "teen culture".

Nick Pollard has written an immensely helpful book called
Why Do They Do That? (Lion, 1998, £5.99) which explores

the world of today's teenagers and will give you information about the way your own teen's school peers think and feel, and the culture with which he or she is surrounded.

When our children are small, their conversation never ceases; my three-year-old son was full of questions and comments about life; he only stopped talking when he was asleep! This often continues right through childhood, but between ten and fourteen something happens; grunts become the order of the day, and you find yourself looking back wistfully to the days before puberty. Many teens do not talk a great deal to their parents about what is happening to them physically, emotionally and spiritually. You may not feel that you have much significance in their lives at this time. (When they do want to talk, it will be just when you are longing for bed; this is the time to ask God for physical stamina as well as wisdom. During the teenage years it's important to "catch the moment".)

You may find that your Christian teenager is talking freely with other Christian adults rather than with you. This can be hurtful, but understand that they are not rejecting you; they are finding that at this time in life it is easier to talk with someone who can view their problems with more objectivity than an emotionally involved parent. But hang in there, they still need you even if they don't admit it! This is a good time, if they are readers, to leave books lying casually around. They may not want a conversation with you about a particular topic, but reading a book is a different matter – just as long as *you* haven't told them to read it.

Emotions (yours and theirs) often run high during the teen years, and extra tolerance on your part is needed. They still need boundaries (twelve- and thirteen-year-olds are often quite relieved to be able to say at a schoolfriend's sleepover, "Sorry, I'm not allowed to watch videos over the 'twelve' category"). We need to know where they are going and with whom. We will already have warned them about drugs and solvents, and the misuse of alcohol; as they get older we have to trust them to recognize the dangers. Money, too, will be a big factor in their lives, and they need to be aware that plastic cards (whether their own or their parents') have to have real money behind them.

Once children reach their teens they are unlikely to discuss sex in any personal way with their parents. Hormones are strictly private! If we have answered their questions and talked to them openly and without embarrassment during their growing years they will have plenty of knowledge, but the hormone surge will make a big difference to their attitudes. We will have given them the appropriate warnings, but we cannot control their lives as they grow to maturity.

There will be times when we need strong prayer support for our teenagers. Attitudes of pride have no place here; we need close friends who are pray-ers and will join us in the battle. One of our daughters suffered from anorexia nervosa for several years; we were heartbroken as we watched her lose weight. We prayed for her and tried, without success, to find out why she would not eat. Her friends at school and at church became concerned as she grew visibly thinner, in spite of the disguising baggy jumpers she wore. Doctors and counsellors seemed unable to help her. We prayed for her continually, and so did several close friends from church who knew about the situation. Finally, God stepped in. Our daughter was attending a Bible Week, camping with the church. She told us that one day, in her tent, God had clearly spoken these words to her, *"How can you destroy your body when I have so much work for you to do?"* That was the beginning of her healing, which took a long time.

Anorexia is a vicious and evil condition, and our daughter later told us that while she was suffering from it she saw a reflection in the mirror which bore no resemblance to the reality. Her slim figure was reflected back to her as an obese, ugly person, and the words "fat cow" came into her mind as she looked at herself. She had felt that she was leading a double life, doing all the "normal" things at school and at church, but fighting a battle with food, self-image and control of her life at the same time.

Teens can be troubled by many things, and at school they will be confronted with those who have made very different choices from their own Christian commitment. A good church youth group can be invaluable, providing a Christian peer group and a forum for discussing many of these choices. They need to hear and discuss truth when they live so much of their time in an environment which actively promotes and teaches relativism.

Keeping a good relationship

It is vitally important to keep a good relationship with our teenaged children. We cannot afford to "major on minors". Green hair, three holes in each ear and a room like a rubbish tip will be neither here nor there in a few years' time but your relationship with your child will last a lifetime, and if you regard these minor matters as crucial, that relationship may be severely damaged. Love the person; ignore the eccentricities!

What if, after all your praying, caring and teaching, your child moves away from faith in God and stops coming to church? This may be due to the influence of school or non-Christian friends, or simply because he or she has doubts and reservations about the Christian faith. There are no guarantees that our offspring will walk with God right through their lives, even though they may have come to faith in him as children. Many teenagers from Christian families opt out of church. Indeed, it is far better for them to be honest about their doubts than to keep them hidden, for whatever reasons; I have known some children of pastors who have lived a double life rather than offend or disgrace their parents. We cannot force faith upon our children; they need to have their own personal relationship with God, based on a real experience of his love and grace in their lives. That has to come from their own desire and commitment, not that of their parents.

If your son or daughter drifts away, God will teach you many things through it; he may deal with your pride (especially if you are a church leader) or your materialism, and you will certainly learn patience and trust. What you need to do is maintain your relationship with your child; keep loving him or her and keep talking. Don't let your children feel that your love for them is dependent on their Christianity. If it becomes obvious that they have got into sinful company and ways, make it very clear that you do not like or accept what they are doing; nevertheless, you love them dearly and nothing will stop you caring for them and praying for them. (Here I want to say something that may be controversial but is my honest opinion: if your teenager is involved in sexual promiscuity, he or she should be given appropriate contraceptive and safety advice; this does not mean you are condoning what he or she is doing – it is damage limitation.)

Releasing our children

We have seen the need to protect our children physically, mentally and spiritually. It is equally important to release them and help them toward independence. Children start wanting independence early. At two years old, "I can do it myself!" is a frequent announcement (usually when you are fighting the clock to get them dressed and out).

We need to check our attitudes toward releasing our children. Some of us find it very tempting to keep our children dependent, needing us and wanting us desperately. God has put the maternal instinct within us to ensure that our children will be loved and cared for with enormous commitment. But an attitude which makes your child the absolute centre of your life will hinder your emotional and spiritual growth, as well as making it difficult for your child to become independent. If this is you, look back over your own history and childhood to find the source of this deep need. Perhaps you were aware of being loved conditionally? Or were you abandoned by those who should have loved and cared for you, let down by those who should have supported you? It is important for you and for your child that you look back over your history and your memories to find the cause of your dependency and need, so that you can seek healing and help.

Protection or over-protection?

Protecting our children is right and appropriate but over-protection can be damaging. The days of *Swallows and Amazons* are over. We no longer allow our children the freedom of playing out unsupervised in parks and fields, or going on long cycle rides alone in the way that children did a decade or two ago, but we need to make it possible for them to enjoy challenge and adventure as much as possible. An enterprising church youth group or outdoor organization, Christian camps and holidays, school journeys – all these allow children who cannot have unlimited freedom in their home area to enjoy outdoor adventures. Camping or youth hostelling as a family will give them new experiences, too, and the anticipation of a camping trip abroad can provide interest for months before it actually happens. We have had several family boating holidays; the Norfolk Broads provided us all with many new experiences! Perhaps you have never been the adventurous type, but ask God for new attitudes for the sake of your children. Help them to find enjoyment in exploring new places, people and ideas.

When our children were tiny, their friends and contemporaries were the children of our friends. But as they grew, their circle widened. Playgroup, primary school and secondary school brought them into contact with other friends, many of whom were not from Christian homes. Sometimes their language and their ways were very different from our own children's, and we felt concerned. But we found that the best answer to this was to welcome their friends into our home and get to know them. Then we could pray for them and be aware of their interaction with our own children. They knew that our kids went to church and that their dad was the pastor, and some were put off by this (or their parents were!), but over the years a number of them came to the church and became Christians themselves. We encouraged our own children to have faith for their friends and to pray for them. It is tempting to want to protect our children from contact with friends we feel could be harmful, but our children have to live in the real world, where they will meet all kinds of people. If we welcome their "wider" friends to our home, it gives us the opportunity to talk with our children about them and about their views on life and how they differ from ours. A welcoming attitude to their friends (and their friends' parents) will be more helpful to your children than a suspicious or fearful one.

Releasing them to make choices

Releasing our children means setting them free to make choices. When they are small we make choices for them in order to keep them safe, but eventually they have to begin making their own. Sometimes this is hard to watch; no doubt you, like me, have felt for the child who spent all his pocket money on a plastic toy which broke half-an-hour later – as you knew it would! As they grow older, their choices will involve clothes, music and computer games; even though we have released them to make choices and our attitudes respect their increasing maturity, we still need to be aware of what our pre-teens and early teens are listening to and watching. You may need to make decisions about whether to object to a child's choices; it is always a good idea to wait and pray before confronting a child with objections.

Releasing our children spiritually

We will always want to pray for our children and to be involved with them but as they grow up we must learn to release them spiritually. Some Christian parents can have a very controlling attitude; they try, by the imposition of "home rules", to keep their children on the Christian pathway. As we saw in the "teens" section, it is better for your children to be honest about their questions and reservations than to live a double life, coming to church to please you but turning away in their hearts because of doubts which they feel unable to share with you. Growing children, especially as they reach their teens, need space to think, discuss and argue. In our house, Sunday lunch-time was a debating forum! We usually had some of our children's friends visiting, and everything from homosexuality to Calvinism was discussed around the lunch table. Everyone was free to contribute and the conversation often helped people to reach conclusions which they may not have been able to think through by themselves. Our children all knew that we would respect their conclusions, even if we did not agree with them.

In Luke 15 Jesus tells the story of the prodigal son. In that story, the father did not stop his son from leaving but gave him the freedom and the money to do so. As our children become older teens and young adults we have to "take our hands off the reins" and resist the desire to protect, control and, most importantly, to criticize. A parent with a critical attitude can destroy the emerging confidence of a young adult learning to make his or her own decisions and take responsibility for them. When one of our daughters was in her late teens God gave me a picture as I prayed for her. I saw a chrysalis which had begun to open in order to release the butterfly inside – but a hand was holding the chrysalis closed. God was speaking to us about relaxing the home constraints and releasing our daughter to live her own life. The time for teaching was over; now it was time to trust her.

Some parents find it hard to release children to become independent, but if you are *always* "there for them", one of two things may happen: they may become a target for bullying because they are seen to be dependent, or they may begin to think that it is always someone else's job to pick them up after a disaster – and this may mean that they fail to take responsibility for themselves.

Before we finish the "mothering" chapter let me recommend a new website. Log on to www.cfnetwork.co.uk and you can link up with the Christian Family Network, which gives advice, help and information on all aspects of parenting.

To consider: In terms of your "mothering season", do you feel that any aspect of "setting boundaries", "teaching" or "releasing" needs attention?

This chapter brings us to the end of the book. I have been challenged afresh in writing it, and I hope it has proved helpful and thought-provoking in whatever "season" you find yourself at the moment. Perhaps you are struggling to adjust to a new situation and finding it difficult; I pray that this book will give you hope and encouragement, and a few laughs as well! Most of all, I pray that it will lead you to trust in God, the Father, the Son and the Holy Spirit, to sustain you through every "season" of your life.

APPENDIX

Introduction agencies in the United Kingdom

The Network
PO Box 20
Braunton
Devon
EX33 2YX

Tel: 01271 817093
Website: www.singleandchristian.co.uk

Choices (for Christian professionals and graduates)
SimpleIdeas Ltd.
118 Piccadilly
London
W1V 9FJ

Tel: 020 7569 6751
email: Choices@SimpleIdeas.net

Christian Friendship Fellowship
Bawtry Hall Christian Centre
Bawtry
Doncaster
South Yorkshire
DN10 6JH

Tel: 01302 711007
email: cff@lineone.net

New Day Introductions
Tel: 01706 224049
email: suenewda@aol.com
www.marriageintroductions.co.uk

Beulah Friendship Bureau
PO Box 17
Basildon
Essex
SS15 5JN

UK websites

www.ukcmp.org.uk
www.christian2christian.co.uk

International website

www.Christian-dating.com

Help for those who are divorced

DivorceCare (UK)
Tel: 020 8534 7339

DivorceCare (USA)
Tel: 800 489 778

Website: www.divorcecare.org

For those in an abusive marriage situation

The Littledale Trust
Littledale Hall
Littledale
Lancashire
LA2 9EY

Tel: 01524 770 266

Association of Christian Counsellors
Tel: 0118 966 2207

(Readers in overseas locations should contact the minister of
their local church for relevant information.)

Useful parenting websites

www.planit4kids.co.uk
For news about children's events and amenities in all areas of
the UK

www.37.com
For help with all kinds of school and homework

www.cfnetwork.co.uk
The Christian Family Network – for help on all aspects of parenting

Notes and Prayers

Notes and Prayers

Notes and Prayers

Prayer that Works

Jill Briscoe's crisp, personal style feels like an honest chat with a wise friend. Basing her teaching upon the experiences of the prophet Elijah, she introduces biblical concepts guaranteed to ignite your passion for prayer. She understands that prayer is rarely undertaken in ideal conditions. So she includes lessons on:

- *The art of leaving things undone*
- *Learning to pray in the middle of the muddle*
- *Sleep deprivation is better than God deprivation*
- *Going through the "wall"*
- *Learning to pray in the dark*

Prayer that Works
Jill Briscoe
ISBN 1 85424 512 0

Available from your local Christian bookshop,
or in case of difficulty contact Monarch Books,
Concorde House, Grenville Place, Mill Hill,
London NW7 3SA, United Kingdom.

MONARCH
BOOKS